James MacGregor

The Land Question. With Special Reference to New Zealand and Old Scotland

James MacGregor

The Land Question. With Special Reference to New Zealand and Old Scotland

Reprint of the original, first published in 1883.

1st Edition 2024 | ISBN: 978-3-38533-277-5

Verlag (Publisher): Outlook Verlag GmbH, Zeilweg 44, 60439 Frankfurt, Deutschland
Vertretungsberechtigt (Authorized to represent): E. Roepke, Zeilweg 44, 60439 Frankfurt, Deutschland
Druck (Print): Books on Demand GmbH, In de Tarpen 42, 22848 Norderstedt, Deutschland

THE LAND QUESTION

WITH SPECIAL REFERENCE

TO

NEW ZEALAND AND OLD SCOTLAND

BY

REV. JAMES MACGREGOR, OAMARU, N.Z.

My kind, now vested with the eternal glory
Of GOD made flesh, glorious to me became.
Henceforth those crowns which shine in mortal story,
It seemed a grief to hear, madness to claim.
To be a man, seemed now man's noblest aim:
His noblest task, to serve one, even the least,
Of those who fight GOD's fight, and share His kingly feast.
— AUBREY DE VERE.

"The first thing the student has to do is to get rid of the idea of an absolute ownership. Such an idea is quite unknown to the English law. No man is in law the absolute owner of lands. He can only hold an estate in them."—Williams, ON REAL PROPERTY, as quoted by De Lavaleye.

"Latifundia perdidere Italiam."—PLINY.

DUNEDIN: JAMES WILKIE.   OAMARU: ANDREW FRASER.
EDINBURGH: ANDREW ELLIOTT.

MDCCCLXXXIII.

THE LAND QUESTION.

BY THE REV. J. MACGREGOR, D.D.

FIRST LECTURE.

At the end of my lecture I find it has come to be a sort of secular sermon, in relation to land, about a nation's right and duty re maintenance of men. And here at the beginning I may throw in, by way of prolusion, what you may regard as a sort of prose hymn about manhood. That may serve to strike a key-note in your hearts as well as mine. There are things known in our hearts which lie there slumbering useless like fire in a flinty rock ; and this prose hymn may serve to awaken the slumbering flame, recalling to recollection what we have had in our hard hearts·from the beginning by creation— the true idea of manhood in relation to nations and to land.

The great fundamental use of land is, Maintenance of men. The true ultimate wealth of nations is, not money, but manhood. What, to a nation, is the use of money but maintenance of men, as many in number and as high in quality of manhood as can be consistently with national well-being and well-doing ? What is a nation but manhood multitudinous, organised into unity of national being and life ? What is its prosperity, at bottom and in heart, but the amount and quality of prosperous manhood multitudinous realised in the sphere of its unity ? What is its life, in the true sense of national life, but the vast harmonious movement of that manhood multitudinous, in manifold oneness of true rational agency, taking form in the nation as organ of the grandest of all conceivable harmonies in this outer court of God's great temple of the universe ? so that when we say, the true use of land is maintenance of men, we assign to it the highest and holiest purpose conceivable in relation to creatures under heaven. For not only in heaven that manhood now shines upon the throne, where it is worn by our God. On earth, too, it ought to shine, as in those whom He has made to be God's kingly priests. As in the universe there is nothing great but God, so, as the poet sings, "On earth there is nothing great but man." And to a nation its manhood is the one thing, lacking which the nation, like a soul without God, has nothing—all its seeming wealth is only a long and vain array of nothings.

After that hymn, I will lay before you as my text the following ideal programme of legislation regarding land. It represents the view that has come to me from study of the subject. I believe it is in substance what is destined to be carried into effect among all free peoples ; and I know that its principles have their roots deep and widespread in the relative constitutional history of nations. But I lay it before you at this stage, not dogmatically, for your adoption, but tentatively, for your consideration. Your present extemporaneous adoption of it would be of little importance. It would be a thing of great importance if your contemplation of it should lead you to serious and fruitful thought about the subject. And for the present it will serve as a text, for convenience of reference in the lecture as a whole.

The first principle here is that the nation, relatively to the land, is paramount lord of all, entitled and bound to make such laws as are best fitted to promote the public interest of the nation as a whole. Then, relatively to the nation's public interest here, the vitally important secondary principle is, that the true use of the land is maintenance of men for the nation. Therefore in legislation about land we must seek a national provision for due maintenance of men, as a fundamental constitution to which all other things in the nation's power must conform. And into that constitution there ought to enter such regulative maxims as the following: —1. Maintenance of men, to the extent and in the manner that are best for the nation's public interest, shall, always and in all places, be a burden on the land, no matter what may be otherwise its tenure of ownership or occupancy, whether public or private. All constitutions and compacts to the contrary, past, present, or future, shall be eo ipso null and void; and violation or evasion of this law shall be branded and punished as a peculiarly infamous crime; but compensation may be made from the nation's public purse to private persons who are made losers through operation of the law. 2. To the extent of the nation's public interest in manhood, and of the land's capability for maintenance of men, those who are willing to occupy land shall obtain it, of such quality, in such quantity, and on such conditions, that a man with fair ability and industry shall be able to maintain himself and his family by the land, in such decency and comfort as are called for by due regard to the nation's public interest in the maintenance of men. 3. The allocation of the land, and the determination of the conditions of settlement, to such men, shall never be left to private proprietors as such, but shall always be kept in the nation's own power, administered by persons appointed by the nation for the purpose, who have no private interest in the matter, but are solemnly entrusted with it, and made responsible to the nation for their administration of it, as a great public interest of the nation.

Having endeavored, by means of this introduction, to initiate a common understanding, or to suggest a general impression regarding ideas and principles and regulative maxims, I now proceed to an exposition in detail, which will to some extent assume the form of notes and comments on the programme that has been read to you as a text. That there ought to be no private property in land, and that landlords ought not to receive compensation for the confiscation of their property by the State;—this is what I have received as a summary report of my lectures in Dunedin. On both points it happens to be precisely the opposite of true. One of the leading points of my first lecture was, that private property in land is perfectly compatible with the programme I have suggested; and that there must be private property in land if there is to be any effective occupancy of it, ex-

cepting that communistic occupation which is barbarously wasteful, and therefore incompatible with due regard to the nation's public interest in land. As to compensation to landowners for loss resulting to them from legislation in that interest of the nation as a whole, I made provision for such compensation an integral part of the programme even in outline, and in the lectures I showed that such compensation could be fairly contended for as reasonable and right. It is not very exhilarating to find my laborious exposition thus read backward like a witch's prayer. But that report, summing up the whole matter in two averments which are both precisely the opposite of true, now does me good service by giving me occasion and excuse for entreating you, in relation to the very important matter in hand, not to strike without hearing, lest you wound me through a man of straw, and fail to see what I am striving to show, for the true interest of landlords and "landless" alike, and for that national interest which equally concerns both.

Te Whiti has gone home from Christchurch, and the Glendale martyrs from Edinburgh, where they have had opportunity, like Jonah in the whale's belly, of meditation on the inconveniences of taking the law into one's own hand. The Maoris, too, have gone away, though not potatoless yet discomfited; and our brethren in Skye, though perhaps "nursing their wrath to keep it warm," are reduced to passive resistance; while their philo-celtic friends and lovers, once jubilant as well as militant in eloquence, are now thrown out into mere sentimental weeping, and wailing, and gnashing of teeth. Captain Sword reposes on his laurels under the sign of the White Horse, and Captain Pen has resumed his wonted leadership of public opinion,— leadership like a wheelbarrow's to the froward child propelling it. Civil war has ended happily, with few tears and no bloodshed, giving place, amid cheers and some laughter, to a sometimes not very civil war of words. Yet, after all this, in these "piping times of peace," here are we, as if on eve of battle, not only "Highlanders, shoulder to shoulder," but Lowlanders, too, as well as Englishmen, Irishmen, and other men in general, assembled in council upon the irrepressible question of the land laws.

"Can't you let it alone? Or try to stop the movement, with its perils to grave interests, especially to the 'sacred rights of property?'" We trust that it shall prove to be perilous indeed to some far from sacred wrongs of property. And in that event, so much the better for the property and its owners. For in a free nation like ours, a wrong at the foundation of property must ever tend to dissolution of it ; making the foundation to be as a quicksand, which cannot sustain the fabric that reposes on it, but may engulf the fabric—if not also those who are housed in it. And in any case it is useless to speak of letting the movement alone. It will not let us alone, nor you, nor anyone. It is fairly under way among civilised free nations, and can never fairly take end among them short of a full ascertainment of truth, and definitive establishment of right as law, such that the law shall make a reign of beneficence on the basis of right. The movement is not that of a rising tide, which will fall again, and leave the vexed shore. It is that of an ever-swelling river, with ever augmenting power, to bless or to destroy. Do not try to stop it. The attempt would be worse than vain. The river might pause for a little ; but only to swell in fulness of momentum, until in angry power resistless it sweep away the barrier of sticks and straw, and perhaps also the mortal creature who has foolishly erected that barrier, against nature and her forces.

But is not this a "high matter"? Yes, it is high :—higher far than party politics and class interests ; higher than political economy and material good ; higher even than political philosophy, with its speculations about civilisation, or completed formation of man as social ; as high as patriotism and philanthropy, on the mountain summits of morality and religion. And we shall look up to those hills for a blessing on our common life and thought here below ; as the land itself, where it sends up its naked peaks into the regions of perpetual frost and snow, there receives from heaven the beneficent streams which run down through all the plains with a blessing and glad song, alike for "palace proud, and hovels of the poor."

But in order to that desired end, we must seek it in a spirit of purity corresponding to the loftiness of the interest in view. We must endeavor, according to our light, simply to seek the truth, the whole truth, and nothing but the truth, for practical guidance in relation to a matter truly high, of world-wide interest to man. In that catholic human interest, I will speak only as I think, calling no man master, though [gladly learning from all who can teach. And I can think only as I see, with such help as I may

have opportunity of finding. If you find that I have not the faculty of vision, then do not accept the guidance of a blind man. But remember that a blind man can feel—and sing, though it should be only a broken fragment of the "auld Scotch songs" of his nation.

I. The fundamental principle, in relation to legislation about land, is, that the nation is paramount lord of all, entitled and bound to make such regulations as may be best fitted for promotion of the nation's public interest. If any one choose to give, to the assertion of sovereign ownership of the land by the nation, the name of "Nationalisation of the land," I will not quarrel with him about his use of a word, though I may think it unwarrantable. But I will here speak to the serious question of fact, whether the assertion of that sovereign ownership, or paramount lordship, in the nation, does not militate against the great institution of private property. And I answer that it does not by any necessity of nature. On the contrary, it is perfectly compatible with the existence and full enjoyment of every conceivable kind of private property compatible with the nation's well-being and well-doing. Yea, with a view to that public interest of the nation, it not only permits, but demands, that there should be private property in land ; and forbids the communistic occupation which some appear to dream about when they speak of the nationalisation of the land.

Communistic occupation means that the nation shall itself be farmer, the only farmer ; while the working cultivators of the land shall be only the nation's captains and regiments of industry, having no personal interest in the produce of their toil. And that, I have no doubt, would be barbarously wasteful. For the nation's economical interest in land, every mode of occupation is bad that will not stand the test of this golden rule : The point of the spade, or heart of the cultivator. Let there be working there the largest possible amount of private personal interest in making the land good, and keeping it good, for production. That personal interest in good soil is the main-spring of good farming, whether with steam-plough or with Hebridean *cas chrom*. On the other hand, communistic occupation makes bad farming, because it destroys that private personal interest in good soil. Thus in England, "common" was another name for "waste." And in Shetland, I have travelled through a district that has for nickname "Arabia Petrea," because it is a barren desert of shingle, sand, or clay; and this not by nature, but through an artistic process of "scalping"—that is, scraping the soil off the "common" land for the purpose of laying it on the private land of garden or farm ; as if you were to tear the "hairy scalp" off an enemy's head for the purpose of thatching with it the bald head of a brother or bosom friend. Communistic occupation of the land is thus condemned by the principle that the nation, as paramount lord of all, is entitled and bound to make laws for the nation's public interest. For in the interest of production, that paramount owner could not do worse than farm the land herself, instead of leaving it to private occupation, with full force of private interest in making and maintaining good soil.

Apart from that communistic occupation, you can see that there is no other kind of effective occupation that does not involve some sort of private property in land. I say effective occupation, as distinguished from a vague and fruitless occupancy, like that by wandering tribes of hunters, or shags, or moas. And, I repeat, putting communistic occupation out of view, every other kind of occupation of the land involves a private property in the land, of some sort or other. Consider what is meant by, what constitutes, property or "own"-ership. "Own"-ership, property—proprium—means, that a thing is mine, and not another's ; so that I have a right, which he has not, to hold it and use it. So far as I have this exclusive right to hold a thing and use it as mine, so far I have private property in the thing. How far that right may go, or how long it may endure, affects, not the reality of private property in the thing, but only the nature of one kind of private property as distinguished from another. Thus, in relation simply to productiveness, freehold pure and simple is best, because it brings the largest amount of private personal interest, in making and keeping good soil, to work at the point of the spade, or in the heart of the cultivator ; who knows and feels that every improvement he makes is for him and his "a thing of beauty and a joy for ever." Leasehold is good, because it brings to the spade's point the cultivator's interest in feeling that every touch of real improvement of the soil is for him and his an investment, in a bank of land, that will bear them interest throughout the duration of the lease. And tenancy at will is bad, because to the spade's point it brings an interest that may work in the way of scourging the

land. But in all these cases alike the holder of the land has a private property in it, in the sense of exclusive right to hold it and use it as his, though it should be only for one year.

It thus is a mistake to imagine that there can be no private property in land except under the form of freehold or perpetual lease. That form affects only the duration of the right. And the existence of the right may be real where the duration is by no means perpetual. Thus not only I have property in my mind through all eternity, and in my body so long as I live on earth in time. Not less really, in the sense now in question—of exclusive right to hold and to use a thing as mine—I have private property in the cab which I hire for half an hour, and in the pencil which I borrow for half a minute. Similarly there is private property in land wherever and to whatever extent a private person has right to hold it and use it as his, to the exclusion of others, no matter what precisely may be the specific nature or duration of the tenure. It may be freehold, making the land to be his free of rent in perpetuity ; it may be leasehold, making it his for a guaranteed term of years with a burden of rent ; or, it may be a merely permissive occupancy of a paddock for one night, to rest and feed a drove of cattle on their way to market. Under all these forms alike private property in land is a fact. And from these illustrations of the constitutive nature of that property, it is abundantly clear that the assertion of a nation's paramount lordship over all, or sovereign ownership of all, is perfectly compatible with the existence, and full enjoyment, of private property in land, under every conceivable form, but one.

But one. That one is one with we shall have a great deal to do at this time ; and with which the nation will have a good deal to do if it is to live and prosper long in the land. I refer to absolute property in land, as distinguished from limited : unlimited power, to "do what a man will with his own ;" such that, for instance, the landowner shall have right in law, by a mere act of his will, no matter what may be the nation's interest or pleasure, to prevent settlement on his land, or expel the existing occupants, and thus far to depopulate the country, or make it empty of manhood. That one kind of private property in land is of course incompatible with assertion of national superiority over all, and of national right and obligation to legislate for the nation's public interest ; because the absolutism of the property, the autocratic power of the proprietor,

places him outside of the sweep of national administration in that national public interest, like Robinson Crusoe on his island :
I am monarch of all I survey.
  My reign there is none to dispute.
From the centre all round to the sea,
  I am lord of the fowl and the brute.

I do not here deny the incompatibility. On the contrary, I affirm it, in the interest of my programme, for it furnishes the foundation of my second proposition.

2. Absoluteness of private property in land, autocratic or despotic power of landowners, ought not to be suffered to exist. And in particular, the nation, as paramount lord of all, ought always to keep in its own power the question of settlement, whether men willing to occupy land shall have the opportunity of obtaining it for occupation, and where, and when, and on what conditions ; and the private proprietors of land, as such, ought never to have that question left to them, so that they shall have it in their power, for their private pleasure or profit, by an act of their will, to prevent population or expel population of manhood ; but that power shall be always administered, for the nation, by persons appointed by the nation for this purpose, and having no private interest in the matter, but being entrusted with it as a great public interest, for the administration of which they, like national officers of justice and war, shall be responsible to the nation, alone.

It is plain that the nation's paramount lordship cannot be asserted effectively, so as, e.g., always to make sure that there is not a ruinous depopulation of the country, if that autocracy, despotism, or absolutism, of private landownership, is suffered to exist. And that, I maintain, is itself a conclusive reason why it should not be suffered to exist. This conclusion begins to commend itself to sound minds as soon as it is stated. It will become more and more clear in course of real discussion— "Truth, like a torch, the more it's shook it shines." And in making it clear, we shall be working for the true interest of private property and landowners. For we shall be laboring for the destruction of one of those wrongs of property which imperil the rights of it, by corrupting the foundation as if disintegrating rock into quicksand. But again, I repeat, while seeking abolition of that wrong, we are far from seeking to weaken—we are really seeking to strengthen, at the solid foundation, the due right of property, in land as well as in everything else.

On behalf of that autocracy or obsolutism in the case of land, we sometimes hear men ask, as if the question had ad-

mitted of only one answer, in their favor, Has not a man a right to do what he will with his own ? To this we answer— No ; a man has not the right now in question—i.e., absolute right, without limitation or qualification, no matter what he may happen to will :—supposing, for instance, he should will, with his own pistol, to shoot his landlord by way of quit-rent. That absoluteness or autocratic power, to do what I will with my own, is not conceded, by the law of nature and of nations, in the case of any other sort of private property. The owner's right is always held subject to limitation—e.g., by the private rights and interests of other citizens, to say nothing of the sovereign right of God over all. There is that limitation, by common consent, even where the thing is mine in the strictest sense—e.g., a limb of my body, or even a faculty of my mind. My hand is my own ; but the law will punish me as a thief if with my own hand I steal my neighbor's purse. My tongue is my own ; but I am punished for libel if I lie away his reputation or his interest. My head is my own ; but it will not long remain my own if I turn it into a workshop of foul treason against my Queen and country. Thus generally, in civilised communities, private property is not absolute ; a man's right to do what he will with his own is not unlimited. And thus the contention for absolutism or autocracy of private ownership of land is a dangerous contention, especially for the landowners. For it exiles their property from the community of all other sorts of private property known to civilised mankind. It places it in a sort of outlawry from the general system or scheme of human society ; thus making it into a sort of Crusoe in society, whose claim to autocracy only exposes him to the danger of being knocked on the head, or confined as a dangerous lunatic.

Further, the question thus raised, between private interest and right on the one hand and the nation's interest and duty on the other, is one that can hardly have a place in relation to any sort of landed property but one—that is, in the case of large estates, estates that are so large that to empty them of manhood would be to affect appreciably the nation's interest in human population of the country. I will not allow the school children to play football in my flower garden. You will not allow a tramp to settle on your paddock, with "a large wife and small family." And in the case of our small properties, the nation has no appreciable interest in disallowing an absolute and unlimited power, so far as human occupation is concerned, "to do what we will with our own." But even in such a case there is always an ideal limitation, which, though ordinarily held in reserve, may, if an occasion arise, be made to operate with decisive effect—*e.g.*, if our private interest in flower garden or paddock be found standing in the way of the public interest in a railway or town park. It thus appears that even in relation to property in land, the question, of public interest and duty against private right and interest, can have place only in the case of those great estates. And here, therefore, we have a further view of the dangerousness —to owners of great estates—of contending for that absolutism of property or autocracy of ownership in their case. It is contended for only in their case. In claiming such absolutism or autocracy of power, to suit their own interest or pleasure, irrespectively of the nation's public interest, and determinations in that interest, they are alone among all owners of private property in the nation. And it is a question worth consideration for them, not simply, is it right, but, is it safe, for them and their estates, to be thus "alone in their glory"—in that condition of alienation or (so to speak) outlawry from the general system of things in the country.

But what mainly concerns us is the nation's public interest in the matter. And in relation to that public interest, we must keep full in view what is the true question now in hand. It is sometimes said that the owners of great estates have themselves an interest in due maintenance of men upon their land ; or, that they will ordinarily show a due regard to the public interest, so as not really to weaken the nation through their exercise of the power of depopulation. Of that I will have something to say by and bye. But at present, what I say is this :— The question is not, whether they are or are not likely to make a beneficent public use of the power, but, whether they ought to have such a power. Supposing, for argument's sake, that great landowners will always and in all cases be perfectly public spirited and patriotic in their action, and always perfectly wise for the nation as well as heroically self-denying in love, a sort of angelic order of men, like, say, the Scotch lairds ; supposing that, is it right for the nation to leave such a power in their hands, and thus to cast it away from its own hands? Would it not be better, wiser, nobler, for the nation to retain the power, and bear the cross of doing its own duty, and win the

thorny Crown of surmounting its own difficulty, rather than allow the business to go into other hands than its own, though it should be of angel or archangel ? And as the matter stands in a world of selfish men, can this great public interest of the nation be safely entrusted to any creature under heaven but the nation itself, acting through its trusted representatives appointed for the purpose ?

In order to see the matter clearly, let us take a very extreme case—as it is by extreme cases that principles are tested. Suppose, then, that a syndicate of Rothschilds, perhaps aided in secret by Continental States, have bought up all the land in Great Britain. Then they have private property in all the land. And the contention is, that in the case of private property in land, a man ought to have power, absolute and unlimited, to do what he will with his own. Well, if Rothschild and Co. "will" that all British men be turned out of British land, have they the moral right to have this will of theirs carried into effect! Are all Britons morally bound to go into banishment from their great old island home of free institutions and nations! Or, again, suppose that, when land was cheap, a "ring" of squatters had similarly got hold of all the land in New Zealand. Would it have been morally obligatory, on account of their thus being owners of the land, to allow them, if they chose, to prevent human occupation of the country, so as to make for ever impossible the day dream of a "Britain of the South." This, you may think, is a monstrous thing ; nothing less than the murder of a nation ; in the one case, by suicide ; in the other, by infanticide. True, but that monstrous thing is made possible by the principle, for which you are contending, of absoluteness in property, or autocracy of rightful power over land, in the hands of a private proprietor. And I will tell you a story— "an ower true tale"—of our time, which will show you how that thing, which appears monstrous and incredible when taken into view as one whole, may be going on in detail, to fatal effect, as if in the natural and ordinary course of events.

The sheep is a very valuable, as well as innocent creature ; and the land, if wholly devoted to sheep, will yield the landlord more money and wool, as well as give him and his factor less trouble, than if it had been made to maintain its due complement of men in fair proportion to its bearing capacity. And the deer is a noble beast, furnishing sport to noble men and gentlemen with full purses and vacant time ; so that the laud, if laid out as a deer forest, may, while giving the landlord almost no trouble at all, yield him more money as rent than if laid out as a sheep farm ;—money that otherwise might have gone away out of the country, to salmon fishing in Norway, or buffalo hunting in the Rocky Mountains, or tiger shooting in Bengal—anything to kill the vacant time. Pondering deeply on these things, the landlord thinks it better that the money should go into his purse. And accordingly, by a simple act of his will, the country is emptied of men, and filled with deer. And the consequence is that, in relation to the nation's public interest in maintenance of men, the land has in effect ceased to be, as effectively as if it had been filled with tigers of Bengal, or sunk into the bottom of the sea.

Look, for example, at the fine island of Jura. It is a deer forest ; not the natural forest, of irreclaimable wilds, but the artificial forest, done to order of sporting noblemen and gentlemen, at the cost of expulsion or exclusion of human population. The few men who are there are there, not as men, but as servitors of the noble beast, acolytes of the sacred order of deer. We can hardly expect that they shall have in their souls a patriotism so great and puissant as to counterbalance the smallness of their number. Relatively to the nation's public interest in manhood, Jura might as well have been at the bottom of the sea as on the surface of it. But such is every deer forest, made conformable to the requirements of men with full purses and empty lives. Insulation—"island making"—seclusion from men, in order to undisturbed repose of deer is of the constitutive nature of that forest. Man may not approach it, so as to see into the sacred preserve. For mankind the forest, though it should be in the richest heart of the mainland, is in effect an island ; an island as effectively as if surrounded by that stormy sea in which the Scylla frightened the shipwrecked sailor into death. Relatively to human population, the land is in effect annihilated, just as if it had been sunk into the profoundest depths of ocean. The deer, if he could speak—like a *foolish ass*—might perhaps say of the landlord, what the grateful Italian rustic said of Cæsar Augustus, *En deus nobis haec otia fecit*—" surely a beneficent Deity has created this repose for us." But Caledonia, weeping for her children because they are not, her true "flowers o' the forest a' wede awa'," may rather say, of the landlord and his sporting confederates

in depopulation, what Caledonian Galgacus said of the heartless filibustering Romans, " They make a solitude, and call it peace"—*Solitudinem faciunt, pacem appellant.*

The solitude so far as manhood is concerned, annihilation of human population, exists not only where there is the deer forest, but also, though not so completely, wherever there is sheep-farming so conducted as to prevent a due amount of human population. That solitude can be produced at pleasure by landed proprietors where the property is absolute or autocratic. And this for the Home country is a very serious matter. Thus in the Highlands of Scotland, the noble Island of Skye is almost all the private property of two persons, Lord Macdonald of Sleat and Macleod of Dunvegan ; the Duke of Sutherland owns not far from the whole of the great country from which he takes the title ; and a very small number of great landowners thus have among them the power of almost completely emptying the Highlands of human population.

If you ask me how the landowning class have used this power, I will now say in passing what I will by-and-bye show at full length. In a century of that power they have made the nation, in respect of manhood, a sufferer to a frightful extent ; so that now the population of the Highlands is not half of what it ought to be in the nation's public interest ; the half that is there are, to a large extent, reduced into a condition of chronic destitution and rack-rented semi-pauperism, in which manhood must inevitably suffer degradation of quality; and the landlords, driving a profitable trade in sheep and deer under protection for which thus they do not pay, are at the same time themselves in some measure supported by so-called "rent" of poor people who have not found it in the land, and in some measure really dependent on that charity of outsiders, which has now and then to make a spasmodic effort to prevent the chronic destitution from running into famine, with pestilence at its heels—and which thus is abused as an insurance to the landowners and their "rents."

But you may suppose for the present that all that is only a delusion of heated fancy. For at present the question is, not about the use or abuse of the power, but about the existence of such a power, in private hands, to use or to abuse at the individual's discretion. Ought there to be any such power, in any hands but those of the nation itself ? Consider its bearing on the nation's public interest. Apart from that solitude we have looked on, the result of that century's experiment may be pictured thus?—(1) Through depletion in respect of amount of population, the nation, the empire, has been bleeding to death. (2) Through degradation of the quality of manhood, the nation, the empire, has been being corrupted in its life-blood, or poisoned in its vitals. And (3) Through mere accumulation of wealth not equably diffused among the community, but here in excess and there in poverty-stricken deficiency, and the vices bred in co-existence of the two evil extremes of poverty and wealth, the nation, the empire, has been languishing into a condition of what may be described as a shameful way of slowly dying, through fatty degeneration of the heart. That, too, you may call a fancy picture, if you will, though some here must well know it is drawn from the life.

The nation's public interest in maintenance of men requires, not only that their number should be sufficiently large, but also that the quality of their manhood should be high. And here you may perceive that the right settlement of the land question for the Highlands of Scotland has an interest for you in this country, at least as deep as it has for the centres of large population in the Old Country. In those centres, which may be called urban districts, they need constant supplies of population from without: recruits to their varied armies of industry, and raw material of future officers of all ranks in those armies; merchants, manufacturers, shopkeepers, artisans, experts in various professions, as well as a numerous rank and file of laborers technically unskilled. Thus, in the American States, the proportion of urban population to rural, which not very long ago was only about 1 to 20, is now, I think, as high as 1 to 4 or 5. Glasgow alone is every year adding some 10,000 souls to the urban population of Scotland, and is not sending out a nearly equal back-stream of population to the country districts. You thus can perceive that even in the Old Country the question of immigration from the rural districts is one of private personal interest to the townspeople, as well as of high public interest to the nation as largely constituted by the population of the towns. It is vitally important that the immigration from the country should be, not only sufficient in amount, but high in quality. And you need only to read the names of leading citizens in the Glasgow Directory in order to perceive that a large proportion of the best sort of population of that great city has been recruited by immigration from rural Scotland,

and this from the Highlands not less than from the Lowlands. And this is as it should be in the nation's public interest. For if the needed supply of immigrants to the urban districts be not supplied from rural Scotland, they must be drawn from some other quarters—as San Francisco is being supplied with "heathen Chinees." And if the population in this way coming from without be of a low quality, the nation is weakened if not corrupted in that working class which is the living foundation of society; with a weakness if not corruption that will, surely though it should be slowly, extend to the society as a whole; as corruption or decay in the root will rise up and spread through the tree as a whole. Immigration of a low class is to the body politic like poisoning of the life blood. And this, I say, has a deep practical interest for you in this new country;—*De te (Zealandia) fabula narratur.*

Upon immigration you are more largely dependent for supply of population than they are in the urban districts of the Old Country. And you, at the outset of your career as a nation, with a people yet largely in a state of solution, have a far profounder interest in high quality of immigrant manhood than they can have in those districts, with their comparatively settled habits and formed character. The character which you require is to be found, let us suppose, in rural Scotland, Highland as well as Lowland. The English historian Froude says that the Scotch, beaten into compact unity as a nation by their long wars of independence with England, have had formed in them a national character which, now in honorable union with England, is worth "mountains of gold" to the Empire. In the interest, then, of "the great future nation" of New Zealand, you well may desire a fair proportion of immigrants from old Scotland. No matter how highly you may think of yourselves, though you should be as "proud an' as great" as "The Laird o' Cockpen," yet for your own sakes—as "wanting a wife your braw hoose ta keep"—you may prudently seek a life-long union with Scotia, "a penniless lass wi' a lang pedigree." Though she have no fortune to sing about, as tempting sordid lovers, "my tocher's the jewel," still, that superlative lass is a fortune in herself, worth "mountains of gold" to the fortunate wooer. Such is your condition.

And here is what may be the condition corresponding in old Scotland. In Lochcarron of Ross-shire, when asked by a minister resident there what I thought of the boys of the district, with whom I had been making acquaintance, I answered, sincerely as well as promptly, that I reckoned them, mentally and physically, the finest raw material of manhood I had ever seen. And of the children of the region, so of the fathers. One stormy evening, darkening toward night, I sailed round Cape Wrath along with 500 Lewis men of Ross-shire, on their way to the season's herring fishing on the east coast. They all engaged in a solemn act of evening worship, conducted in Gaelic by one of themselves:—beautiful reading and prayer, and song which, mingling with the storm, was really sublime. As they rose up to the prayer, reverently baring their heads, what struck me most, looking on from a higher part of the vessel, was the magnificent array of shaggy heads and broad shoulders; and I felt that I should not like to be in an enemy's war vessel boarded by such men, fearing God, and just and true to man. Such a combination as they exhibit, of sterling good character, good education, and robust physical force of manhood inured to perilous toil, manifestly makes a quality of manhood that would indeed be worth "mountains of gold" to a new country such as this. And I suppose that here and elsewhere in New Zealand, and all over that empire on which the sun never sets, wherever there are Scotchman —and where are they not?—the empire sees cause to rejoice in the Highland as well as the Lowland *alumni* of the "wise auld Scottish nation." But what if the fine gold become dim? What if Scotia brave and free have sunk into a spiritless and slovenly slave? What if the manhood of the Home country be lowered in quality? Then it is not only the Home country, but the whole of the great British Empire, and even that "Greater Britain" which includes our American cousins, that is, as a body politic, thus far poisoned in its life blood.

The blood-poisoning, of a lowered quality of manhood, may be brought about in various ways. For example, by forced and unnatural emigration. "Emigration" is the cry whenever there is a peculiarly urgent pressure of the chronic difficulty about the land question. And the cry is sometimes a heartlessly selfish one : men merely seeking evasion of a problem which they have not the heart and head and hand to solve. They seem to regard emigration as a matter of course, if only it serve as a temporary make-shift for putting off the evil day of settlement. But it is not a matter of course. And as

a make-shift for such a purpose it is worse than useless to the nation. Why should men emigrate, so long as there is fairly room for them in the land of their birth, unless it be by their own free and deliberate choice? There is a natural emigration, which, like charity, is twice blessed, to giver as well as receiver ; being the wholesome process of spontaneous departure of surplus energy, like the swarming of bees from an over-full hive. That, while pleasant to those adventurous youthful bloods who go, is at the same time wholesome to the community that remains. But a forced and thus unnatural emigration, though it should in the first instance benefit the colonies, tends in the long run to injure even them, through blood-poisoning of the Empire, by lowering the quality of manhood, in those magnificent breeding grounds of men, on which the colonies are so largely dependent for supply.

You know what is meant by scourging the land through excess of production beyond fair bearing capability. There may be scourging of animal life as well as of vegetable soil. The Shetland pony ought to flourish in his own "Lofty Land" of storms. But of late there has been a sensible deterioration of the breed. A prohibition to employ women and children in a certain sort of labor in mines occasioned a great and sudden demand for the ponies to work in place of them ; where, I was glad to hear, our sturdy "poor relations" are thriving remarkably. But in the meantime their successors are fading in their old home. The sturdiest, of course, were taken away ; and they were taken in such excess, over the natural supply of vigorous sires and dams, that the progeny of their punier compatriots are now not so good a breed as there once was. Similarly there may be deterioration of the breed of men, scourging of manhood, through emigration that is forced, unnatural, excessive. If, as may be expected, the ablest and best men, who have the power and the enterprise, go away ; and those who remain are the comparatively feeble, physically and mentally, who have not the means, or have not the spirit and energy, to go ; then a deterioration in quality of the remanent manhood is plainly inevitable, through sheer necessity of physical causation.

But the manhood of the country may thus be scourged into degradation, not only by the draining of a forced emigration, but also by straining of privation or toil. My Lewis acquaintances had in their favor certain moral and spiritual influences favorable even to physical well-

being and well-doing; as Godliness hath
the promise both of this life and of that
which is to come. But there may be
physical conditions that natively tend to
sure though it should be slow deterioration of manhood even morally and
spiritually. Though they should be
created by mere will of man, as when a
man gives a slow poison to his neighbor,
they operate with the force of natural
law. The grace of God will do much to
counteract such evil tendency. In an individual it can do almost anything, short
of the physical miracle of antidote to
poison. But in a community, whose life
extends over generations, we are not entitled to expect that, through counteracting influence of that grace, we shall not
reap as we have sowed if we impose or
tolerate physical conditions that are de-
grading in their nature. The grace of
God will not prevent the soil from
running to waste, if, in addition to
scourging it with excess of cropping, we
starve it by giving it no manure and little
sun. Nor will that grace for ever keep a
human population from deterioration in
quality of manhood, if the people be
chronically under physical conditions, of
want or toil or both, natively tending to
depress and degrade.

It thus is idle to talk vaguely of giving
the people the land to live upon. In
order to guard the nation's interest in
manhood, the people upon the land must
be so placed upon it, under such conditions, that they shall be able to live upon
it, in such a measure of decency and comfort that the manhood in them may not
be under a natural necessity of degradation. Give an Irishman, in fee-simple
for ever, a small patch of bog, and you do
not make him a prosperous freeholder,
but degrade him into a bog-trotter, and
bind him down, as truly as if you had
made him formally a serf, into perpetual
degradation as a slave of the soil. In
order that the manhood may be such as
the nation has need of, the man who is to
live upon the land must have it of such
quality, in such quantity, and on such
terms, that, with reasonable ability and
industry, he shall be able to maintain
himself and his family in decency and
comfort.

And here again appears the vital importance of the nation's reserving to itself
the sovereign power of determining the
questions regarding settlement, of human
population: how much of it ought to be
upon the land, and where, and how in
respect of conditions. We have heard of
the evils of "free selection,"—that men
left to themselves will select what is un-
suitable even for themselves; or that
they will so select as to ruin great estates
by misplacement of population and cultivation. And it is sometimes said, as if it
bore upon the present question, that there
is some land so ill-placed for human
population that, even for the nation's
interest in manhood, it were better to
leave it with deer that can live upon it
than occupy it with men who cannot fail
to starve upon it. That may be quite
true. But the question is, who is to
judge and determine in the matter? And
I answer, not the private owner of land,
with full power of law to shape the matter
simply for his own interest or pleasure,
but the nation, prescribing for the nation's
public interest in due maintenance of
men. The nation, in that public interest,
can forbid human occupation of land that
is not really capable of maintaining men.
The nation, in that public interest, will
prescribe such limits to free selection that
the individual's choice of a site for his
farm shall not be allowed to injure the
general productiveness of the district in
which he settles. But, also and especially,
in that public interest the nation will not
suffer autocratic landlordism to impose such
conditions, of bad land, small quantity,
high rent, that the occupants shall be a
population, not of prosperous manhood
such as the nation needs, but of over-
toiled, half-starved, rack-rented semi-
pauperism.

Here, too, it is important to observe,
that circumstances of depression and
degradation, which we may be disposed
to ascribe to natural peculiarity of race,
may really have been caused by physical
conditions created by man, and may arise
in the history of any race that is sub-
jected to the conditions. Thus the Hu-
bridean Islanders, of Celtic race, Gaelic
in speech, and originally holding their
land under a system of tribal ownership,
find themselves in certain economical circumstances of depressing poverty, under
the autocratic power of lairds, or lords of
the land, come in place of their chiefs of
the clan. And we may imagine that the
circumstances are the result simply of
constitutional peculiarities of Celtism.
But the Orcadian Isles are not Celtic, but
Scandinavian - Teutonic. It is not long
since they spoke a Norse tongue there.
And the system under which the land was
originally held there was the extreme
opposite to the clan system: it was that
Udalism, which is the extreme of individualism, of freehold pure and simple.
In respect of race, there thus is a marked
contrast. But in Teutonic Shetland the
circumstances of depressing poverty are

to a large extent the same as in Celtic Lewis or Skye; for, under the autocratic power of landlordism, the physical conditions are to a large extent the same.

Since the original preparation of this lecture, there have come to hand the newspaper reports of an examination in Skye, by a Royal Commission of inquiry into the condition of the Highlands and Islands. There we have the evidence of the poor Hebrideans themselves regarding the true causes of their chronic poverty, now and then amounting to such destitution as to call for a spasmodic effort of public charity for prevention of starvation. The causes set forth by them are mainly, too little land, too poor a quality, insecurity of tenure—for that is what they really mean by saying that they would like to have no landlord but the Queen. They set forth also, that, as they cannot wring a maintenance from the land, they have to try to eke out the produce of it from the sea, and that the consequence is, bad farming and bad fishing. One of them says, If you be both a farmer and a fisherman, you are bad at both. Yes, but there are the same causes, producing the same effects, in Scandinavian Shetland. I have spoken of the barbarous waste of their "scalping" the soil off land held in common by townships. And I might speak of a similar bad economy in their custom of run-rig, which may have some advantages, but which has the fatal disadvantage of diminishing the amount of private personal interest working at the end of the spade. But now I will take only one illustration from their mixed practice of fishing and farming. One evening in Shetland a gentleman said to me,—"The truth is, that our people will never do well the farming of their crofts; for they are fishermen, and their hearts are at sea." Next morning, I read in the local newspaper,—"A splendid shoal of cod was this week sighted off Scalloway; but the boats did not go out to catch them, as the men were busy planting their potatoes." Thus in Teutonic Shetland as in Celtic Skye, if you are both a farmer and a fisherman, you are bad at both. And the same point is further illustrated by comparing the Orkneys and the Shetlands, the two groups of those Orcadian Islands themselves. While the Shetland Islanders are in circumstances of depressing poverty like that of the Celtic Highlands and Islands, the Orkney Islanders are comparatively comfortable in their circumstances, like the mainlanders of Caithness and other Scottish Lowlands. And why? There may be more than one

reason for the difference. But here is the reason that was given to me by the Sheriff of the County of Orkney and Shetland (Mr Thom); viz., that while in Shetland there is the mischievous combination of croft-farming with sea-fishing, in Orkney there is happily a severance of the two industries; the farmer is only a farmer, and the fisherman is only a fisherman; and the consequence is, good farming and good fishing, and prosperity of men.

Moral: As to the land, let those who occupy it have so much of it, of such quality, and on such terms, that a man can live by farming alone; and, let the nation see to this. Otherwise, the nation has itself to blame if its rural population be in circumstances such as the following:—The people, though for long voyages the best sailors in the world, and, both male and female, extremely laborious in their home lives, are yet extremely poor. It was brought out in sworn evidence before a Royal Commission of inquiry into their truck system, that many of them almost never have coined money in their hand, and that three-fourths of them are always in debt:—on the wrong side of their landlord's book, who pays them only in kind, of goods at a price fixed by him, for their fish at a price fixed by him, and which they must bring to him, because he can at his pleasure turn them out of their crofts (if not into gaol). As for the women, whom you meet on the way with a "keeshie" load on their backs and busy knitting in their hands; they, in like manner, go with their Shetland goods to a "merchant" who pays them in draperies, with which they have to go to some other shop for purchase of groceries, or other such necessaries of life;—fancy one going with a bonnet as purchase-money for tea and sugar!—And I was told by the late Dr Cowie, author of the now standard book on Shetland, that women in Lerwick, the capital of those islands, who on Sabbath would appear in church as well-dressed and well-conducted as his wife or daughter, or mine, would, to his knowledge, during their week of hard work be literally pining with hunger. That is under a system which the nation can destroy with a breath.

There is one aspect of the possible results of that system which, though happily not now presented in Scotland, must be glanced at in passing, no matter at what a cost of feeling of painful revulsion. Here is a description of the result, as once apparent in Ireland, by the famous traveller and observer, Arthur Young :—" A landlord in Ireland can hardly invent an order which a servant, a laborer, or a cottar dares refuse to execute. Disrespect, or anything tending toward sauciness, he may punish with his cane or horse-whip, with the most perfect security; a poor man would have his bones broke if he offered to lift his hands in his own defence. [Mr Young has here a further detailed illustration, which might wound the feelings of some readers, and of which the accuracy has been questioned in a manner deserving respect. The quotation is therefore thus far left incomplete.] Nay, I have heard anecdotes of the lives of people being made free with without any apprehension of the justice of a jury." (In the Contemporary Review for April, 1883—"Irish Murder Societies," by Richard Pigott.)

Are such things likely to occur if landlordism be autocratic? No: and slave-drivers are not likely to be such villains as Legree; and monarchs, if despotic, are not likely to be monsters like Nero or Phalaris. But the question is, whether the owner of private property ought to have, not only the temptation but the power to do such things, at the cost of cruel degradation to the manhood of a nation? His having such a power is itself a deep degradation to those over whom he has it; and, while the shame is mainly theirs and his, the sin is also the nation's, which suffers any such power to be in any private persons' hands.

We now clearly see that the nation's interest in manhood requires provision for the land's maintaining, not only a sufficiently large number of men, but also the highest attainable quality of manhood, in the rank of personal cultivators of the soil. We are told that the population of the Scottish Highlands is now somewhat larger than it was before the clan system was abolished, and the chiefs became lairds. But it now may not be half so large as it ought to be. And though the amount had been large enough, or too large, yet, if the quality be lowered, the nation may be really weakened instead of strengthened. Suppose, for instance, that through deer-foresting one-half of the Highlands is depopulated, as if the land had been sunk into the sea. Then the nation is not strengthened, but weakened, if the population thus displaced be so placed on other land, that the other half shall be over-crowded with rack-rented semi-paupers, on barren moors or in squalid sea-shore hamlets, driven by want to wander far, like crows or gulls, to gather from a distance on land or sea the subsistence, for them and their young off-spring, which they cannot find in their "homes"—for which they pay "rent" (!) A nation of which the manhood is so placed, to any considerable extent, may have wealth, in sheep, and deer, and cattle on a thousand hills. But it cannot have health, and is not in the way of long life in the land; but is in what I have described as a shameful way of slowly dying of fatty degeneration of the heart, as well as poison in the blood.

3. Absolute property in land, autocratic power in landowners, is a dangerous innovation in the constitutional history of our nation relatively to land. I might show that it is alien to the primitive historical constitutions of nations in general, especially those of the Japhetic or Aryan race to which we Celts and Teutons alike belong. But for present purpose it suffices to show that, relatively to the constitutional history of our own British nation, the thing is an innovation of the worst sort, a power for evil that has crept into existence through inadvertence, having no root in any recognised principle of law, but being the unfortunate "accident of an accident." Of landed property in a civilised society there are three, and only three, conceivable forms—individualism, tribalism, and nationalism,— which in our history are represented respectively by the Udal system of the Orcadian Isles, the clan system of the Highlands, and the feudal system which has prevailed so widely over all the British isles, and left so many traces among the modern peoples which inherit the civilisation of ancient Rome. And I say that the absolutism, that now is contended for as if it had been "a sacred right" of property, is essentially antagonistic to all those systems, as existing in our constitutional history, and thus is condemned by them all as a wrong against the "law of nature and nations."

Here observe that I raise no question about the public policy of great private estates in land, with an aristocratic class of landowners. That policy may be discussed, for and against, on other grounds. Thus, with reference to the current of population from country to town, with no equal back-current of transition from town to country. That is everywhere to be observed, not only in Great Britain, but in the 'Greater Britain" which includes our Colonial Empire and the United States. Even in our own young colony, almost wholly dependent on the land, while there is a constant movement of country people into the towns, there is not a nearly equal disposition of townspeople to go out upon the land. There may thus be a danger to our new civilisation from excess of urban population over the rural. Urban populations are naturally democratic, with the vices as well as virtues of a democracy. And it may be desirable to have in the community a class of great landowners, resident on their estates, and coming to have in them that aristocratic type of character which is naturally formed by the position of a territorial grandee in the dignified seclusion of his own domains : — partly in order to counter-balance the evil tendencies of democracy pure and simple ; partly, because the aristocratic type of character has a certain value of its own ; and partly, because the mere variety of types will serve to augment the nation's wealth in amplitude of picturesque variety of social character and life. So it may be contended. And against that contention I at present have nothing to say — no interest in saying one word. For the aristocratic class of great landowners can exist without making property in land to be absolute or un-limited ; and in our own history it has so existed, alike under all systems of Udalism, clan, and feudalism, which have all had their territorial grandees, while all existing without autocracy in owner-ship of land by private persons.

Of the clan system I will here only say a passing word, because I expect to speak of it more fully in another lecture. I will only say of it that, as in the case of Maori tribal ownership in New Zealand, under it the sort of absolute power now contended for not only did not exist, but could not exist ; was simply impossible if not inconceivable. The modern landlord who tries to play the chief, speaking bad Gaelic, and strutting about in kilt and plaid, with "a hundred pipers, an' a', an' a'," stands to the real old chief of a clan in no real relation but one of con-trast, involving anti-climax. He is not a civil and military leader of men, but only a more or less foolish dealer in land. And if he be clever, and yet assume some airs of a chief while contending for autocratic power of modern landlordism, he is to our view only as the "red fox," which was sung of by Ossian "sweet king of song," as prowling amid the ruins, peering through the casements, of the desolate palace of Balclutha, where heroes had in old times listened to min-strels at the feast of shells in lofty hall. Let us pass from that paltry anachronism, of paltriest "Heelan' pride."

At the furthest extreme from that tribalism is the individualism which, his-torically pictured to us in the Shetland udaller, shall here and now be repre-sented for us by our own freeholder pure and simple. The udaller had "no supe-rior under heaven." A very fine thing to say : and true enough thus far, that he had not over him any such intermediate superiors as might, under the clan system or the feudal system, stand between the individual and the whole community. But in the banker or mortgage company our freeholder may have a superior—over heaven?—whose face might quell the fiercest pride of individualism in Scan-dinavian Berserker ; and who may be far less considerately good and sympathetic in heart than a landowning prince of his people like the Duke of Buccleuch, or a laird with a chief's heart like Cluuie Mac-pherson. And further, the freeholder always has a superior in the nation, to whose authority he must submit unless he will become an isolated individual, an outlawed, "broken" man. That nation will make him pay taxes for his property in land, as well as for any other kind of property. It will burden his land for maintenance of men—say, soldiers, judges, ministers of religion—to any ex-tent it may deem desirable in the nation's public interest. It will oust him from his estate, if it see cause, for crime or for debt. Or, though there should be no such cause, it will take from him —with due compensation, let us hope—either a part of his estate or the whole of it, if that should be deemed requisite for the nation's public interest in a railway or town-park. Free-hold pure and simple thus has nothing in its nature to countenance the contention for autocracy or absoluteness of pro-perty in land ; but has very much of use and wont to condemn the innovation.

The only remaining system of tenure of land by private persons is the feudal. In England, too, the very existence of a large part of the private property in land is of comparatively recent creation. A very few generations ago the "common" land, which has been gradually enclosed and made the property of landowners, was more extensive than all Scotland, included nearly half of all the soil of Eng-land. The feudalism which has so widely prevailed has not obliterated that fact from our history, nor the traces of it from existing English practice. But to feu-dalism I now refer, especially because it has by some been regarded as a strong-hold in support of the autocratic land-lordism of our new time, while in fact it furnishes very forcible illustration of contrast to this landlordism. And it is all the more important to mark this con-trast of the systems in their heart, because there are some surface resemblances of the two which, concealing that contrast beneath, may appear to furnish some countenance to the modern innovation of autocracy.

"Let arts and commerce, laws and learning die, but leave us still our old nobility." The creature (I refrain from naming him) who omitted this incredible piece of folly has, let us hope, come to be a wiser and perhaps a sadder, as he is a much older, man. He cannot have known that "the old nobility," about which he sang with "scrannel pipe," was one to which the autocratic individualism claimed for modern landlordism would have been, if not mentally inconceivable, yet practically a monstrous absurdity, or a revolting political paradox. For feudalism meant nationalism, in relation to land as well as to life. According to the new landlordism, relatively to human population of the land, the nation, with its public interest, and its determinations in that interest, ought in effect to be nothing, in order that the private owner, with his interest or pleasure, his will, should be "all in all." Of the old and true feudalism, on the contrary, it was the distinctive genius, the constitutive essence, to make the nation, with its interest and will, to be "all in all," and the individual, even the highest, to be nothing except as means in relation to the nation as an end. Hence the peculiar place of the "crown," or monarch, as standing for the nation, the paramount lord of all. The great feudatories, holding in the first instance from the Crown (i.e., nation) might in their turn have subfeudatories, holding lands from them as vassals. The land was held on condition of military service (afterwards commuted into some equivalent). And that service had to be rendered by all and sundry, according to their various places and ranks in the hierarchy, from the lowest of those vassals up to its culmination in the King. And the meaning and effect of that mode of tenure was, to make maintenance of men, in condition for military service, not only a part, an essential part, of the system, co-ordinate with other parts; but really the fundamental purpose of the system, to which all other things had to conform as subordinate. The system in its essence was constituted by the principle, that the land is occupied by the nation as—like bees in their hive—an army of occupation; and thus maintenance of men, to the extent of the nation as an army of occupation, was by the system made the one great fundamental use of the land.

I here leave out of view the here irrelevant fact of villenage and serfdom. The villains and serfs were, in the old feudal times, regarded as not properly part of the nation : as under the patriarchal system there were bond-servants, and even servile tribes (e.g. M'Raes, servants of the MacKenzies), who though in the clan, were not of the clan; and as there were great masses of population which had no place on the roll of citizenship, but were reckoned as "things which are not," in the freest of free states of pagan antiquity. We, in the advancing light and life of Christian civilisation, have gradually expanded in our conception of the nation, so as to include in its citizenship the whole mass of the people of the land. Again, I do not now go into the question, how the the theory of feudalism, that the land is for maintenance of men, could be held alongside of such practices as that of the forest laws, which in those old times were so grievously oppressive in effect. No doubt the theory, with all its true nobility of spirit, was marred in application through an alloy of ignobleness of selfish men ; and under the system a wide margin was left, unguarded for oppression, in that class of common men who under the system were not owned as properly part of the nation. But under the old system the noble spirit, of nationalism, really lived and moved : as truly at Runnymede as at Bannockburn ; as truly when the barons bold were with mailed hand wringing the great charter from paltry King John, as when Robert Bruce, with a battle-axe, was inculcating his views of Scottish rights upon the thick bull-head of Henry Bohun. Regarding those barons, here are the words of the greatest commoner our Empire has ever seen, addressed to their successors in the Chamber of Peers :—"They did not confine to themselves alone that great acknowledgment of national rights which they had wrested from the sovereign, but delivered it as a common blessing to the whole people. They did not say, These are the rights of the great barons. No, my lords: they said in the simple Latin of the time, *Nullus liber homo* (' no free man '),—uncouth words, and sounding but poorly in the ears of scholars, but they have a meaning which interests us all. These words are worth all the classics. Those iron barons, for so I may call them as compared with the silken barons of modern days, were the guardians of the people." (William Pitt, Earl of Chatham :—Speech in amendment of the Address, 1770. In Timbs' "Lives of Chatham and Burke," p. 133.)

Making due allowance for inadequate conceptions or realisations of what constitutes the nation, and taking into view the nation as recognised then and there, we perceive that the system, in its fundamental constitutions, really did make the nation to be "all, and in all." It made maintenance of men to be, not only a high public interest of the nation, but tantamount to maintenance of the nation's very being, as a force in military occupation of the land. It made the greatest feudatory to be, not properly a private owner of the land, entitled to use it at his mere will for his pleasure or profit, but rather a public trustee, administering the land as a national estate, and therefore bound to have it always, through due maintenance of men, in a condition of preparedness for defence or defiance, at the bidding of the nation. Realisations of this ideal were frequently far from satisfactory as such. But the ideal was there, in genial formative operation. This must be said in justice to a system that has been ignorantly blamed as well as ignorantly praised. Through all its iron rigours, there shines upon the historical student this nobleness from the heart of it, that the great idea of the nation, as the be-all and end-all, pervaded and dominated the system throughout, as an imforming spirit of life, like the soul in the body, "all in the whole, and all in every part."

Hence details, which when now seen in isolation present an aspect of repulsive harshness or cruelty, are, when regarded as parts of the system, redeemed by being seen to have that nobleness, of all-controlling regard to the nation, in the heart of them, as in the heart of the whole system. Primogeniture, for instance, and entail, in isolation as they now are, may well appear to us hard and cruelly unjust to younger children, as well as injurious to society as a whole. But in the old time they were not, as now, applied for the purpose merely of perpetuating a pampered line of do-nothing lords or gentles, in the interest of paltry family pride. They were applied to a public purpose truly noble. That purpose really was, to provide that the nation's public interest should be guarded here securely. And this purpose was sought by preventing the resources of the estate from being frittered away into imbecility through division and subdivision among many individuals, and arranging that they should always be held in forceful concentration, along one well-defined line in one strong skilled hand; and that in this way the nation, at every hour of need, should have in that position a trusted and capable

defender, to wield its resources there with the forceful freedom of a disciplined habit, and authority of right long descended and unquestioned, as well as high heroic motives of ancestral *noblesse oblige*.

The spirit of the system, as animated by the great idea of the nation, is well illustrated in our own old border history of Scotland. The tribes along the border were far from exemplary in formal subordination to the central government at Edinburgh or Stirling. And they often had fierce private wars and furious feuds among themselves. But there is no other thing in our national history more remarkable than the manner in which, if the nation should be seriously threatened from without, those seemingly wild tribes promptly flew to the defence of it. If only an English army of invasion came and looked across the border, then, no matter what may have been the dear delights of fighting, or other occupations or recreations, at home, the Scott, or Kerr, or Hume, or Douglas—whatever great lord happened to be nearest with his force—he at once went straight with his force to place himself and them as a shield between the hostile sword and the nation's heart. And this was ordinarily done with promptitude swift and unhesitating, as if it had been felt, not as a matter of painfully oppressive obligation, nor as one of high but difficult public duty, but as a matter of course, in relation to which there is no occasion for hesitation or delay, as there is no possibility of doubt. That is very remarkable. Another thing in that old history is perhaps equally so. That is, the manner of those who relate the story, in prose or verse, in annalistic writing or oral tradition. They do not speak with wonder, in terms of admiration, as in the case of a thing really not common, about that sacrifice for the nation, that complete self-surrender to its interest and will, which to us is so striking on the part of men ordinarily so fierce in imperious self-will. They refer to it simply as a fact, in the manner of one who does not see anything to wonder at, and is not in the least aware that yonder deed, of battle unto death for the nation, of self-devotion to death for the nation, by the chief and his followers alike, has in it anything but mere matter of course. Such in reality was "our old nobility."

The spirit of modern autocratic landlordism is thus of a wholly different species from the spirit of a true feudal chief, "that fine old English gentleman, all of the olden time." It is indeed a modern spirit, of the basest sort, masquerading under ancient if not antiquated forms. In respect of exclusive regard to private pleasure and profit, to the exclusion of the nation's interest and right to rule, it is essentially that same spirit which animates a "ring" of Yankee speculators, in sordid worship of mammon, banding together for the purpose of preying on the common-weal, so that, while carefully keeping clear of the hangman, they may rise and shine as "bosses" or millionaires, To one desiring to "honor all men" there is nothing more saddening than that modern illustration of "the deceitfulness of riches," that gilded but most foul dishonor to true manhood, the worship of the "almighty dollar." There is no more sad *finale* of sordidness to a human career than a strong man's paean over "success in life," "Soul, thou hast much goods laid up for many years: take thine ease, eat, drink, and be merry." There is no more shameful suicide of manhood than is involved in the self-devotion of an able man to that "success" as the end of his life's career. The highest success here is a ruinous failure. The "man made of money" is—like Jerrold's terrible picture of one literally turned into bank-notes—a man unmade by money, self-debased to the dust to which he cleaves with his poor soul, sunk beneath the materialism of the Mammon which he worships, a rational being who glories in the shame of being a very highly prosperous mole! But in the romancing imitator of feudalism the shameful degradation is peculiarly revolting. We have spoken of the sham clan chief as the "red fox" prowling in the long desolate ruins of once lordly and festive Balclutha. The sham feudal chief —to what shall we compare him? Shall we say, to a bloated spider that has crept into an old hero's helmet on his tomb? Certainly the grasping autocratic landlordism of our new time stands related to the heroic nationalism of the feudal system in "the brave days of old," as the bloated spider to that hero,—in relation of despicable, loathsome, hateful, profoundly humiliating contrast.

I now repeat the statement made at the beginning of this section of my lecture. Individualism, tribalism, nationalism, are the only three forms of property in land that have ever existed in our country, or that are known to the history of mankind in civilised society. The autocracy is alien to society in relation to them all alike; and therefore is in effect condemned by them all alike as an outrage on the "law of nature and nations." From the view-point of the constitutional history of

mankind in relation to land, it falls to be regarded as having no real root in any sound principle of law, and thus being only the unfortunate "accident of an accident"—while practically it is a dangerous innovation, profoundly revolutionary, subversive of the very foundations of civilised human society.

It is important to observe at the same time, as a fact shining along the whole face of our past history, that the modern autocracy is by no means necessary to the existence of great estates, or of an aristocratic class of great landlords. The destruction of it would only remove from their property a burden—of power to depopulate—that is dangerous to them and to the nation, and replace it with a burden " of obligation to due maintenance of men" that is salutary to both. Such a burden on the land, of obligation to maintenance of men of certain classes, is made familiar to us by the case of national establishments of religion, with their church rates and tithes. Such a burden in relation to ordinary settlement of men willing to cultivate the land for a living, is made familiar to us in New Zealand by the nation's action towards leaseholders of great estates as sheepruns, in covenanting for a reserve of power in the nation to break up the sheepruns into small farms, in a manner deemed wise and good by the nation. And, I am given to understand, even in the case of freehold, an obligation to allow what settlement of men the nation might think wise, was part of the original constitution of great landed estates in Canterbury. There is, in truth, no reason why it should not be so. Nothing, I mean, in the nature of the thing, private property in large estates, encouraging the manners and tastes of an aristocratic caste. Such a caste existed in ancient Athens, and in the Italian Republics of the Middle Ages, where the aristocrats were in habit not like our great landowners resident on their estates, but rather like our merchants who are princes. But if you will have great estates, consider what has been said of the clan system and feudal system. Under both systems the modern autocracy of landlordism was really inconceivable; and—as a burden on the land — maintenance of men, to the full amount required by due regard to public interest of class or nation, was not only permitted and secured, but practically regarded as the one great purpose of the existence of the land—yes, and of the chiefs. And were not those old chiefs of a sufficiently pronounced type of aristocracy ? It is well if the aristocracy of Chatham's "silken lords" be in effect a gaudy and flimsy imitation, hiding a ludicrous contrast, to the warlike glories of his "iron barons," or to the simple grandeur of a true old Highland chief.

What I say, then, is, *Delenda est Carthago.* With a view to the nation's great interest in manhood, ample in quantity for the nation's purposes, and as high in quality as legislation can provide for, the autocracy of landownership, vile innovating upstart, has to be destroyed. Let the nation resume the power, and always exercise the power, with vigilance and trenchancy unsparing, of guarding that interest as she would guard her life. If not, then, though matters should present an aspect of prosperity, yet, in relation to the very foundation of a nation's life and strength in manhood, the body politic may be sinking into fatal fatty degeneration of heart, or becoming poisoned in blood through degradation of the quality of manhood, or, through undue diminution of the number of men, perhaps here and there in unregarded extremities, be bleeding to death. And let the work be done, not from deference to merely sectional democratic impulses, whose cries may be no better than "blatant blockheadism," and whose spirit may be merely that of hard and scraggy selfishness, but from due patriotic regard to those principles, relatively to the interests of the community as a whole, which were incarnated, under forms adapted to the times, in the clan and feudal systems at their best. In this way the landlords themselves shall be relieved of their dangerous burden of autocracy; and the movement, in breaking off their chains, tearing off their grave-clothes of that innovation, will be really in effect most beneficent toward them, and truly give us back "our old nobility."

And for that "old nobility" brought back, there may be a really great career in our new time. I have spoken of the progress of our Christian civilisation, in leading men more and more to regard the whole community as within the pale of proper citizenship of the nation. That progress, in bringing manhood as such to the front, has in some measure superseded the old nobility of circumstance, in favor of an older nobility, which, indeed, is the oldest and truest nobility, of nature. The nobility of circumstance are thus, by such a formed free nation as ours, no longer needed as they once were. Their place and power as leaders of mankind are coming to be more and more occupied by commoners like William Pitt, and William Ewart Gladstone, whom Robert

Burns would describe as "noblemen by creation of God Almighty." Still, a Hartington may have in him the older or oldest nobility of nature, the title to lead that is constituted by possession of "the kingly governing faculty." And if he have this, his power for noble ends is greatly enlarged by what he has in his old nobility of circumstance,—prestige of inherited honors and high rank, as well as the material resources and varied social influences of the heir of a vast estate. So long as the world stands, with its firm abiding unity in endlessly interesting variety of human population and circumstance and feeling, our great landowners may continue to have a great opportunity, of leading as their fathers led, though in a different fashion because in different times. Lord Elcho, now Earl of Wemyss, may serve his kind as truly in watching over the farmers and hinds on his great estates in East Lothian as when he did such splendid public service in organising the British army of volunteers. The present Duke of Sutherland finds ample for his remarkably great force of character as well as wealth, playing a true Duke—dux— "leader" of men, in a very different sort of "Sutherland clearance" from some we have heard of,—in labors of Hercules for bringing a railway to the Pentland Frith, and transfiguring wide regions of barren waste into gladsome fruitful soil for maintenance of men. If only our noblemen and gentlemen by rank be in reality manly men of heroic type, like him, taking a lead in great beneficent enterprises for the nation's good, then the "red spectre" will never so much as look in through our windows, and we shall not be seriously discomposed when deafened by the braying, though we may be disgusted with the hard and scraggy selfishness, that sometimes goes masquerading under the abused name of Democracy.

What is bred in the bone will come out in the flesh. You see that I have taken to preaching, in relation to the present and future, and am giving way to Celtism in my leaning towards the days of old. Why should I not ? The evils in our view are caused, not simply by want of thought, but also by want of heart. And the heart is benefitted when the mind is made to dwell on what was good or great in the past. Then the past comes to live anew among us, "though dead, yet speaking," with a power to us in the present which truly is a river of the water of national life, flowing in Providence from the throne of God everlasting. And now let me reward your patience by showing you, in conclusion, a picture from the past, which I showed some time ago to the people of Columba Church, Oamaru.

I have spoken of a "ring" of paltry American adventurers preying like foul birds upon their nation's life. And in derisive scorn I have spoken of another "ring" of the same sort, as formed ostensibly on behalf of "old nobility," but really for sordid selfish class purposes, of men proceeding upon the view, that the land with all it contains is for them. Why should not they, and we, proceeding upon the view, that they and we are for the land and all that it contains, form a very different sort of ring :—a ring, a gold-be jewelled ring, of honest patriotic citizens, banding together for promotion of the nation's public good? That is what we all ought to think of, and long for, and make for:—not the degradation, from natural place of dignity and power, of any one class, whose existence is not proved a dangerous nuisance; but the elevation of the nation in all its classes; or, better still, by all its classes, banding and battling together for the nation's well-being and well-doing under God. For those who are of this mind I will now show the picture I have spoken of. It is of a ring, a gold-bejewelled ring, that once was formed by our Scottish forefathers, standing "shoulder to shoulder," "red wat-shod in blood;" while all sought and fought for the common good, and everyone found occasion to feel that "the rank is but the guinea stamp; the man's the gowd, for a' that." The picture is done by a master hand, and, one might say, with the heart's blood, of one who loved the "old nobility," perhaps "not wisely, but too well," but who loved his nation as became one bearing the "kindly" name of Scott. The ring he depicts was formed round James IV. of Scotland, on Flodden's fatal field; when "the wise auld Scottish nation," driven to bay, unwavering and unshrinking confronted pale Death; and the valiant "Soutars o' Selkirk" fought and fell abreast of lordly Douglas "tender and true,"—the desperate rampart ring that never was broken, but melted away in advancing shades of death and night ("Marmion," vi., 34):—

The English shafts in valleys hailed,
In headlong charge their horse assailed ;
Front, flank, and rear, the squadrons sweep
To break the Scottish circle deep,
    That fought around their King.
But yet, though thick the shafts like snow,
Though charging knights as whirlwinds go,

Though bowmen ply the ghastly bow,
    Unbroken was the ring.
The stubborn spearmen still made good
Their dark impenetrable wood,
Each stepping where his comrade stood,
    The instant that he fell.
No thought was there of dastard flight ;
Linked in the serried phalanx ti_ht,
Groom fought like noble, squire like knight,
    As fearlessly and well ;
Till utter darkness closed her wing
O'er their thin host and wounded King.

Glorious defeat ! Yes, and having in it seeds of a victory as glorious. Giant England, in 314 pitched battles, with skirmishes and sieges, in the long wars of independence, succeeded in hammering and welding the Scottish people into a nation compact in unity of strength and soul and heart. Thus was formed a national character which, according to English Froude, has proved to be worth "mountains of gold" to the empire. And from the long baptism of fire, undergone by princes and people in common, there emerged a social benefit perhaps greater than the political. That is, men learned to love and honor as brethren all who had gone along with them through the flames. So it came about that Scotland was thinking, not only of her "princes and lords," but also, and perhaps especially, of her "bold peasantry," her crofters and cottars and burghers, when she raised her long-remembered lament over Flodden and her "flowers o' the forest, a' wede awa'." And their descendants have come to love her with that proverbial passion of affectionate veneration, which inspired Walter Scott as truly as Robert Burns, and which, all the world over, even at the remotest antipodes, makes them love to look on the face of a "brither Scot." To all true citizens of this most noble British nation there is a great career, with fulness of happy occupations well-beseeming nobleness, for all their heart and soul and strength and mind. This career is open to the "old nobility" of circumstance, as well as to the older or oldest nobility of nature. Only let them, thus noble men by rank or genius for rule, be manly men who love their kind with manly heart. And, were it only in order that as noble leaders they may ever have meet noble following, let them fill their native land, not only with sheep and deer in due place and proportion, but, above all, with a prosperous valiant manhood, like that which burned and shone in him who, peasant-born but Heaven-inspired, claimed to be "a nobleman by creation of God Almighty."

SECOND LECTURE.

Themistocles, when laughed at for the badness of his music, said it was true that he could not play the flute, but that he could make a small state into a great one. One does not need even to be a practical politician, to say nothing of political genius like that of the Athenian statesmen, in order to be able to utter a warning about a danger which he has seen that may be of advantage to his nation. The warning which I now proceed to address to you is about the growth of a upas tree, under whose deadly shade the British nation has in some respects been languishing to death. And it is now addressed to you, whose nation has to a considerable extent a *tabula rasa*, *carte blanche*, or clear open field for legislation about land, happily free from complications which have risen to older states from inheritance of constitutions that have lost their good and gained an evil in the room of it, as a body which is wholesome and lovely when in life becomes a loathesome and dangerous nuisance after death. And to you it is addressed in the hope that you may seek, through timely use of your power as citizens of the nation, to prevent that upas tree from growing up among you to blight your future as a nation, or, if it have to some extent grown up already, to destroy it when tender and young, before it have become old enough and strong enough to destroy you as a people. There are evils which in the germ hardly appear to be evil, or may appear to be good. The upas tree in germ may not be very clearly distinguishable from a tree of life, whose leaves are for the healing of the nations. And, relatively to this, a young nation engaged in laying the foundations of the future, may obtain a vast advantage, the benefit of experience without the painful cost of it, if only it study the warnings of history of older states, so as to learn from the distant and the past.

The upas tree is autocracy of property in land, or absolute or despotic power of right in private proprietors;—such, *e.g.*, that a landowner shall be able, by his mere will, irrespective of the nation's interest and will in the matter, so far as his land goes, to depopulate the country; as, for instance, at this hour a very small number of private persons have it in their power, by law, to depopulate almost all the Highlands of Scotland. In another lecture I have shown that the autocracy or absolutism of landownership is by no means necessary in order to existence of private property in land, or of large estates in the hands of private individuals; that such absolutism or autocracy has had no existence either under the feudal system, or under the clan system, or under the udal system—under any form, of nationalism, tribalism, or individualism, of landownership, that ever has had any root of principle of law in the constitutional history of our nation relatively to land; that the autocracy of modern landlordism is a dangerous innovation upon our whole constitution relatively to landed property and every other sort of property; and that, in especial, an obligation to maintenance of men upon the land, at the nation's discretion, and to the amount and on the conditions prescribed by the nation, that this obligation, so far from being incompatible with the maintenance of private property in landed estate, great or small, is fully compatible with the existence and enjoyment of every kind of landed property conceivable in civilised society, and was amply and nobly illustrated as a fundamental constitution of the two great historical systems of tribalism under clan chiefs and nationalism under feudal chiefs. And now, in the present lecture, I will endeavor to illustrate the positions that have been exhibited in the more abstract form of general discussion, from the pathetic history of the Scottish Highlands as bearing on the interest of the Empire.

It may be said in this relation, the things which you propose in your programme to be done by the nation through its law, are or will be done by the landowners of their own will. To this I answer—first, in that case they ought to have no serious objection to have things prescribed by law. Second, we do not want to have these things done by the will of private owners of land; we want them done whether they will or no; we want them to be placed high and and far above the mere will of individuals, and solemnly undertaken and provided for by the nation magistratically, as things vitally affecting a great national interest, transcendentally superior to all personal or private inclinations of individuals or families. And, third and last, we know from a long and painful experience of our nation, that this great national interest, which the nation cannot let out of its own hands without shame, cannot with safety, without great appalling peril, be left in the hands of the private owners of land.

The experiment was made in circumstances most favorable to the justification of landowning autocracy by the result. The Highland proprietors had the strongest imaginable reasons for being just and generous to their tenants in the use of the autocracy secured to them by law. The land had really belonged, not to the chiefs, but to the clans. The chiefs had been, not lords of the land, but leaders of the men. They, like other gentry of the clan, might have separate estates of their own, with tacksmen, crofters, and cottars under them. The chief, besides, for his maintenance in state, of both peace and war, might have certain reserves of the public land, and certain tributes or rents from land appropriated to clansmen. Still, *quâ* chief, he was not, like our modern lairds, a lord of the land, but only, like a Maori chief in the North Island, the leader of the men—sometimes only the elective leader, within the limits of—so to speak—the royal family of the tribe. The clan was paramount lord of all. And the clansmen, whether as tacksmen, as crofters, or as cottars, under the broad constitutional shield of the clan, had rights of property in their holdings, whether as owners or as tenants, independently of the will of the chief. These rights of theirs were simply destroyed, by an act of the national will, after the suppression of the rebellion under Charles Edward Stuart in 1745-46. The hereditary jurisdiction of the chiefs was abolished. The clan system was broken up. And they who had previously been chiefs, leaders of the men, were now exalted (or degraded) into lairds, or owners of the land. Further, the clansmen, having in this way so strong a claim upon them in justice, had a peculiarly strong and tender claim upon their affection. For by common consent they were of the chief's own blood; so that their very name—of clan—meant "family"; and his designation — *ceann-cinneach* — meant "family head" or "patriarchal ruler" of his children.

It might therefore have been expected that these new landlords would show themselves perfectly safe and trustworthy keepers of the nation's great interest in manhood; that on their lands, at least, there would always be plenty of good men for the nation. Although it had been so in their case, it would by no means have have followed that it is safe and wise universally, or ordinarily, to trust an autocratic power over population in the hands of private proprietors, who may have an interest, or a perverse irrational pleasure, in depopulation. But in fact the experiment, in that most favorable case for the autocracy, in a century has resulted as follows :—(1) The population of the Highlands is not half of what it ought to be in the nation's public interest. (2) Of the fractional population that there is, a considerable proportion are so ill-placed upon the land that it cannot maintain them in such decency and comfort as would be compatible with maintenance in them of a high quality of manhood. (3) The landlords, partly supported by rack-rents, scraped together by semi-pauper tenantry from outside of their holdings, are partly dependant on public charity, in the shape of occasional spasms of endeavor to keep the poor tenantry from starving—endeavors which thus operate as an insurance for the laird and his "rents."

I have already referred to the general fact, that at the end of the century of autocratic landlordism the population of the Highlands has not diminished, but augmented, since the beginning of the new regime. That fact has been appealed to, by some who ought to have known better, as if showing that the reign of lairds has been a good one for the country. But, Canning said, "There is nothing more fallacious than figures—except facts." And it is easy to show the fallacy of the "fact" now in view. In point of logical cogency, to prove the thing alleged on the ground of it, it needs only to be steadily looked at in order to disappear from view into nothing—like a *boluch glas* of imagination or of mist. For, (1) The augmentation, where it has taken place, may have taken place, not by reason of favoring influences of autocracy of landlordism, but in spite of malignant influences of the same, through favor of other influences counteracting the malignity. (2) Though the population over all have been augmented, and in some places it is too great for the public good, that does not justify total annihilation of population in some places through deer foresting, and a depopulation really detrimental to the public interest of the nation through a certain sort of sheep farming in other places. Charles Lamb, when blamed for always coming late in the morning to his work at the India House, humorously excused himself on the ground, that he always went away from it early in the afternoon. But the humour of this making "two blacks" into "one white" is out of place in relation to a matter so grave as right settlement of the land question. And if half of the Highlands be emptied of men, and the other half be over-crowded, then in this case to plead growth of population as justification of the reign of lairds, is to say in effect, that two blacks make one white. And (3), and above all, though the population should now be a third more than it was at the beginning of that reign, yet the reign is shown to have been a disastrous one if it be true, as it can be proved, that the population ought to have now been at least double of what it then was.

The suggestion, that the population of the Highlands all over ought at least to have been doubled, needs only to be considered in order to be seen to be feasible. The population of Scotland all over has, within the same period, been more than doubled. Her wealth has vastly more than doubled; so that her average wealth per citizen, which at the union was ludicrously below that of England, is now above that of England. The Highlands, then, if they had economically progressed at the rate of Scotland as a whole, would have had about double their present population. But the rate of progress in the Highlands ought to have been greater than that in Scotland all over. For the Highlands ought to have benefited in larger proportion than the Lowlands from a century of great improvements in agricultural science and art, and in facilities for internal intercourse of commerce as well as for coasting navigation;—improvements, that is, in respect precisely of those conditions which have most to do with a country's capability for maintenance of men. That century has in the Highlands been characterised remarkably by a reign of peace: a peace so profound that an armed man is never seen there unless it be a soldier at home on furlough on peaceful visit to his friends; and the policeman has hardly ever any business except to try to look busy and important; and serious crime is almost completely unknown. The rural districts of the Lowlands have, no doubt, especially the purely pastoral and agricultural districts, been, in considerable though not equal measure, similarly blessed with peace; lions in the field have there too been lambs in the fold; in the Lowland parish where I first was minister, during the four years of my ministry a policeman was never seen on serious duty re crime but once, when he was hunting after a thief who was supposed to have passed through the parish on his crooked way of life nefarious. But the Lowlands, it must be remembered, had long before "Charlie's year" been a comparatively settled country; though the patriotic Fletcher of Salton maintained there were 200,000 "sturdy beggars" or tramps, who ought, by way of abating the nuisance of vagabond idleness, to be caught and turned into slaves. In the Highlands, on the other hand, the century's reign of peace had come after centuries of almost unbroken reign of war, which must have been economically desolating as well as incessant; as witness the following little "fact,"—In the precincts of Balquhidder church, a few yards from Rob Roy's grave, there are three or four fine old plane trees, which are singular in this respect, that there are no other trees in the region of nearly equal age with theirs; and I was told by the late excellent Mr Macgregor, the minister of the parish, that they had been planted about the time of the union of the crowns under James VI. of Scotland and I. of England, and that the reason why there had not been many other such trees planted in the region in that age was, that the age was so disturbed with wars as to be unfit for peaceful occupation such as planting. There were feuds within the clans themselves, and a normal state of private war of clan with clan, interrupted by lucid intervals of union of the clans in rebellion against the central government of the nation. Economically, therefore, the breaking-up of the clan system after the last rebellion was to the Highlands a vast advantage; so that the regime of the lairds there, for which it is only claimed that during the century the population has grown to the extent of perhaps a third more, while it cannot be denied that much of this population is in a condition of chronic poverty involving constant peril of starvation—that regime falls to be regarded as demonstrably disastrous.

And here let us pause to consider what, for the nation, is the woeful significance of disaster such as that. Our sense of the disaster is embittered by the circumstance, that it occurred in a period of peace highly favorable to population :—

It was not in the Battle :
No tempest gave the shock :
She sprang no fatal leak ;
She c me upon no rock.
But his sword was in the sheath,
And his fingers held the pen,
When Kempenfeldt went down,
With twice four hundred men.

Nor is the bitterness alleviated by the recollection, that the lairds, who once had been chiefs, were under peculiarly strong obligation of justice and honor, and blood relationship, real or supposed, to use their autocratic power in the manner most favorable to prosperity of the people, who had been made "landless" by the act which made the chiefs into landowners. But let us look at the disaster as it is in itself, apart from the circumstances of pain and shame in its origin. And let us look at it only from one restricted point of view,—that of national economy.

Of questions of strictly agricultural or pastoral economy, regarding the best methods of farming on hill or plain, it would be ridiculous for me to give an opinion of my own ; though I may by and by give you the opinion of really qualified experts. But I may speak with a good grace, and you can hear with intelligent appreciation, about questions of what may be called general or ulterior economy :—what, on the whole and in the long run, will be most conducive to a nation's prosperity so far as dependant on land. You and I know, for instance, as well as any farmer can, that scourging the land, though it should enrich him, will impoverish the nation ; and that our Scottish proverb, "The mair greed, the less speed," will find illustration in his case if, in his eagerness for present advantages, he neglect the permanent improvements represented by fencing, and drainage, and manuring. Well, in relation to the nation's ulterior economy, there is occasion for application of the maxim given to the world long ago by one who did not prophecy where he did not know : "There is that scattereth, and yet increaseth ; and there is that withholdeth more than is meet, but it tendeth to poverty."— (Prov. xi. 24)

In my former lecture I spoke of the properly transcendental value of manhood itself, such that undue diminution of the number of men, or lowering of the quality

of manhood, is a loss to the nation in respect of that highest and noblest wealth, as compared with which mere material wealth is nothing more than sheep and deer would be to tigers of Bengal. It falls to me habitually to inculcate as truth of God, that in respect of this highest and noblest wealth the nations can never fully prosper except through belief of that Word, the belief of which by the peoples has demonstrably been the instrumental cause of our modern civilisation to the peoples. But this is not the place nor time for that kind of teaching. Even the Bible history of land legislation, with its curiously interesting and profitable lessons of human sagacity and goodness under guidance of Divine inspiration, is not available for my present purpose ; because the land laws of the Bible were intended, not for universal application, but for the special case of the Jews in Palestine, under pupillage and in training for a special purpose, demanding constitutions that might not be suitable to the rest of mankind. I will speak of economy only as related to material good. And in this relation I will speak of it as demanding men for the ulterior purposes both of protection and of production.

1. Of production I will say only a few words. I refer not only to the primary production, of agricultural and pastoral industry, but also, and especially, to the secondary production represented by manufactures and commerce. It is needless to dwell upon the vastness of the extent to which this may tell upon a nation's wealth. Some years ago I became aware that after a very bad harvest in Britain, in one fortnight there came from foreign countries into the Port of Leith as much corn as would keep all Scotland in bread for the winter ; so that the people had bread, where there otherwise would have been probably a famine—possibly a revolution—if the natural supply of food had been intercepted by mischievously grasping protective legislation. In Mr Bertram's "Harvest of the Sea" you can read that in the German Ocean there are 30,000 square miles of good fishing ground ; and that of that vast sea-farm every acre could, on the average, yield without impoverishment, year after year, six times as many tons of fish as the best corn land in England will yield of wheat. It is now near a generation since I somewhere saw the statement that machinery in Britain was producing an amount of manufactured goods equal to all that could have been produced by 800 million pairs of human hands—i.e., a number considerably larger than that of the whole

race of adult mankind now alive on earth.
I need say no more of the vast importance
of manhood for the secondary production
of wealth, and of the vital importance of
having that manhood high in quality.
A very little reflection will enable you
to see that a nation is on the way to
beggary in so far as its population sinks
below what it well could be ; and would be
on the same way of shame and sorrow
although its population, remaining
high in amount, were to be lowered in
quality; so that for sailors we should have
—say, Lascars, instead of Shetlanders
making the long voyage ; and "heathen
Chinees" instead of those artisans whose
clear and masterly dexterity has made
Britain the model workshop of the world;
and perhaps South Islanders, brought by
man-stealers pretending to be employers
of labor, or a debris of shiftless loafers
from the Continent of Europe, instead of
ploughmen like those of Berwickshire
and shepherds like those of the Scottish
mountain land. It was recently calcu-
lated that, as every British human being
is economically worth, on the average,
L100 to the nation, so the annual emigration of 150,000 souls means a loss to
the nation of L15,000,000 a year. Of
course where the emigration is natural,
and therefore wholesome, the loss directly
will be made good indirectly, like a man's
expense of vital force on wholesome and
productive labor. But the calculation—
oddly prosaic though it be in aspect—is
well enough fitted to show the badness of
a national economy that does not provide
for due maintenance of men.

2. Protection—I mean, protection, not
against the nation, but for the nation's
wealth ; not against wealth from without,
but against war without and fears within.
Against fears within, security, so important to prosperity, is possible only where
the population is high in quality as well
as large enough in amount. For, to say
nothing of elements of danger within a
low-class population itself, there is ever
an ideal possibility of wars from without,
to which commercial and manufacturing
enterprise is keenly sensitive, so that a
vagrant rumor of war may cause a commercial disaster to the nation. The merchant vessels, bringing wealth to our
shores, are truly like the fleets of ancient
Sidon, as doves that fly to our windows,
with messages and pledges of peace from
beyond the sea. But beyond the sea
there are ironclads, possible armadas,
against which we must be and feel secure
in order to enjoy the fulness of inward
prosperity ; and against which we can
never be nor feel secure unless we have

plenty of good citizens who can be turned
into good soldiers.

Political economy, teaching truth regarding methods of attaining to material
wealth of nations, does not teach the
whole of truth that may be requisite for
our guidance even to that end. For instance, she teaches, Buy in the cheapest
market and sell in the dearest. And for
ordinary purposes this is, no doubt, a
lesson of truth, of beneficent truth ;—that
in our self-regard we should practice that
"benevolent neutrality,"—"for a consideration"—giving away our surplus
goods to those who have most need of
receiving them from us, and relieving of
their surplus goods those who have most
need of bestowing them on us. But there
are cases in which this maxim of non-
heroic virtue does not apply. Take the
case of a besieged city, with provisions
running short, and consequent peril of
being driven to surrender by starvation,
with clear conviction that surrender means
death or "chains and slavery." Unless
the citizens be mad with blind accursed
greed of gold, no amount of rent will in-
duce them to set apart as pasture for sheep
that space within the walls which is
needed as standing and fighting ground
for men. And, though the enemy would
joyfully purchase the lessening provisions
for a thousand times their market-price
anywhere else, yet the clever citizen, who
shall take them out and sell them in that
dearest market, will be, not lauded as an
economist, but hanged as a traitor. A
nation will similarly entreat the smart
citizen who shall break through the
blockade that shields his nation's life.
Now the British nation, among the nations
of the world, may find itself at any time
blockaded or blockading. And in order
to be and feel secure against wars from
without, it must always hold itself in preparation to assume, if need be, the atti-
tude and action of defence, or defiance, or
assault which may be the best method of
defence,—as Scipio saved Rome in Italy
by destroying Carthage in Africa.

It thus is not enough, even for enjoyment of material good, that we have it.
Unless we have it scarcely guarded, we
can hardly with strict truth be said to
have it,—not to speak of enjoying it and
multiplying it. Rather it may be said to
have us, as timid apprehensive votaries,
who tremble at the rustling of a leaf. A
full purse, a good digestion, a clear business head, and even a kind neighborly
heart, will leave him a despicable weakling,
and no man, who, in a land full of
robbers, has no strong armed hand to
shield or strike. And so of the nation.

We as a nation are very much on the sea with our great wealth. And we may find ourselves very much at sea with it in another sense, like a whale among sword-fish, if we have not plenty of men who can and will fight, among hungry nations that can and will. So said the London Times once about Italy and Austria :— Italy is all prey, and Austria is all sword. And our great British nation, with all its admired wealth, may find itself as helpless and despicable as a "great whale," among a shoal of hungry sword-fishes. The sword-fishes, no doubt, will all practice a severe self-restraint, of "benevolent neutrality," and "act from a maxim fit to become law in a system of universal legis-lation," and pensive leave the whale to go in peace. At least, if we can believe the blessed pacific philosophers of Manchester. But though we could believe them, we could not, I trust, endure the shame of acquiescing in the conclusion, that our nation ought, in the confidence of the kind consideration of other nations, to leave itself helplessly dependent on their mercy. That were an impoverishment indeed, and beggary in respect of what is best worth having in a nation. The amount of mere material good that it is physically possible to enjoy, is comparatively limited ; and to that amount—thank God —mere material good is fairly within reach of all classes of citizens of this nation alike. Beyond that, the good which we have in the nation is mainly constituted by sentiments connected with nationality—the feeling and view of its happiness and grandeur in the pre-sent, and the heart-filling memory of its glories, in success or defeat, through the long eventful past. But if, in the way suggested by Manchester philosophy, of peace that is infamy, our nation sink into a despicable weakling, then for us— Ichabod—the glory of citizen-life is de-parted, the memory of the past is only a sting of reproach for present baseness, and all the wealth of "bloated armaments" that are unarmed is only a transparent gilding to the shame.

Instead, therefore, of such philosophy of infamy, we shall listen to fiery-souled poetry, to which indignation gives its verses of sorrowful scorn. And first, let us hear gentle Goldsmith, lamenting over his "Deserted Village" :—

Ill fares the land, to hastening ills a prey.
Where wealth accumulates, and men decay.
Princes and lords may flourish, and may fade ;
A breath can make them, as a breath has made ;
But a bold peasantry, their country's pride,
When once destroyed, can never be supplied.

Then, at the end of that poem, in a part-ing invocation to the "Muse," he resumes the plaintive strain, until the lyre is grasped from his hand, and the song is carried to its close, by strong-hearted and great-souled Samuel Johnson :—

Aid slighted truth with thy persuasive strain ;
Teach erring man to spurn the rage of gain ;
Teach him that states of nature strength possest,
Though very poor, may yet be very blest.

Here, where gentle Oliver waxes weak, strong Samuel breaks in with a peroration of proud indignant warning. "Teach him," he cries, unmelodious, but ruggedly noble in strength,

That trade's proud empire hastes to swift decay,
As ocean sweeps the labored mole away ;
While self-dependent power can time defy,
As rocks resist the billows and the sky.

"States of nature strength possest." "Self-dependent power." Mark the words ! The poets here are wise—vates—sacred bards, whose poesy is prophecy. For, as we have said, the true ultimate wealth of nations lies, not in dollars, but in men. The nation that will be strong, so as to stand in the evil day, and having done all, to stand, must rely, under God, not upon its money, but upon its man-hood, its own fundamental strength, of robust life, upheld and sustained in itself against all assaults without, like pine of Clan-Alpine :—

Moored in the rifted rock,
Proof to the tempest shock,
The firmer he roots him the ruder they blow.

Such a tree is the nation that has a pros-perous valiant manhood at its basis. That basis, or root, or living foundation, is at the same time the fountain of life, in robust fulness like its own, to all the noble tree, which rears its proud head from the forest, and laughs at the storm. On the other hand a rootless Christmas tree, laden with rich gew-gaws, and perhaps having a sham protective armour of dead branches and mock prickly spears, —there is the wealthy but effete nation-ality that has not in itself the manhood of that "native strength," which would have made it a "self-dependent power"; for the world if possible,—against the world, if necessary.

You will not have a nationality like that ? Very well : you must look to the land for men that can serve as the nation's shield and sword. And in order to see them there when you look for them, you must have them there, in good condition, at all times. What, then, do you see on the Highland hills of old Scotland, where you once had an eminently warlike though peaceful race of men? Here we come to the second part of our pathetic story of misrule.

Soon after the first beginning of the wholesale evictions, the then Glengarry, no longer a chief but a laird, accidentally stumbled on some smugglers in the solitude which he had made, as a way (they say) of peace for his wife, who had quarrelled with the clan, and could not bear their company on the land. The "broken men" seized him, and handled him roughly. The agitation of ruffled dignity occasioned to the dignitary a momentary lapse of memory; and, forgetting he was not a chief, he cried out for "his men"—to the rescue. "Call for your sheep, man," said one of the assistants, "the men are in America." It was a sad thing to say, even for that "salvage man";—that the men, the gallant simple clansmen, with all their happy fulness of picturesque variety of life, and storied memory and song, were gone for ever, like a dream of the vanished past, far, far from their own old famous "land of bens, and glens, and heroes." It was, perhaps, sadder for him for whose ancestors theirs would have exulted in fighting to the death :—in that old home of his people, where they would all but have worshipped his ancestors as demigods, there to stand naked and helpless, in a solitude broken only by a few skulking law-breakers, and be made to feel that even to these he was only an object of loathing contempt, as the dishonored scion of an honored line, who had sunk from their loftiness as leaders of men to the mean villainy of a man-selling trafficker in sheep. It was saddest of all for the nation. It was the nation that had given to a creature the power, when tempted by wife or devil, to banish a gallant race of its children from the old ancestral homes of their hearts. It was the nation that had, not only thus begun to bleed to death, but itself been the guilty author of the wound. It was the nation that had stripped her children of their defensive armour, of inherited right to remain in their homes. It was the nation that had put the lethal weapon, of legal power to banish them from their native soil, in the hand of a creature whom it placed under no responsibility for action so fatal. And the nation may yet have cause to lament its crime, its criminal stupidity, with a repentance all too late. A day may come, of battle sore and dire, perhaps for national freedom or life, against overwhelming odds, a day of desperate extremity, in which the nation, crying out for "men" to the rescue in that agony, shall be answered from the mountains by the bleating of innocent sheep or the belling of dun deer, instead of the *tha 'tighinn foyham éiridh* that should have shaken a thousand hills, the mustering war-cry of the bravest of mankind.

Here is a plain, practical test of the truth, and sincerity of the suggestion sometimes ventured on more or less obliquely, that after all there has been no such mismanagement of the nation's business of population as will seriously affect for the worse the nation's high interest in that business. Let the lairds— *qua* "*chiefs*"—call for "men" to the nation's defence. At first it was possible here and there to "raise" a regiment for the service of the King. For the old habits lingered some time after the old constitution had departed. Not a few of the lairds retained a chief's heart toward the clansmen whom they had retained on their land. But gradually new times gave occasion to new manners. "The stars in their courses fought against Sisera." And Sisera—the new lairdocracy — perhaps did not fight much against the stars, or swim very strongly against the "stream of tendency," which the new law had created and was sustaining in their interest. They no longer had need of men, to be their strength in war, and their crown of joy and glory in peace. But they now had sore need of money, to sustain them in that new gentility of landlordism which had come in place of the old simple grandeur of chiefs—a gentility expensive, and ever tending to slide into shabby genteel. And money, much money, could be made by putting sheep, or deer, or other such higher animals, into the old immemorial place of men. And so the men were "cleared" off the land, as troublesome cumberers of the ground, which their fathers had held by tenure of the sword after they had won it by their sword and spear ; to go to distant lands, or anywhere else out of the way. And when the best of the men had thus gone away, with a rankling sense of wrong in hot Celtic hearts, those who remained, with the misery and shame of remaining, were not likely to show much of a fruitful enthusiasm in responding to the war-cry of a laird, to whom it was only dishonor that his fathers had been chiefs—*cinne-cinneach*—"family heads," to their fathers.

And now let the process be "tested by results." Here and there it was long before the results were fully seen. There were landlords who strove in the new position to maintain the old patriarchal relations of chief to clan, and occupy the land as if the tribal ownership of clansmen had remained a reality, in fact though not in fiction of law. And that feeling on their part was meetly responded to. And a clansman has in him the making of a patriot. So, even in our time, during the great wars at the beginning of the century, Skye, it is said, sent to fight the nation's battles 10,000 soldiers, as good as any the world has ever seen. And brave Fassiefern, when he fell at Quatre Bras, was at the head of a regiment of Highlanders brave as himself, "tough as the heather, strong as the pine," and true as heart of oak. But now the men of Skye, when questioned by a Royal Commission, will bitterly mock at any word of their being soldiers, whose spirit is broken and crushed with a poverty shameful as well as woeful. It is doubtful whether it would be possible to "raise" 500 soldiers in Skye by any form of appeal. And if the form should be that of lairds calling for "their men" as chiefs, it is certain that the appeal would, over the Highlands as a whole, be met only by derision as a ridiculous anachronism, such that even the energy of hatred has died out of the scorn that once met Glengarry in, "Call for your sheep, man : the men are in America."

The sad result thus suggested was inevitable. On the one hand, the chiefs of old, whether patriarchal or feudal, had real need of the men. They were his volunteer army, and the fundamental part of his wealth. For him to expel them would have been to empty his purse and throw away his sword and shield, and set his house and fields on fire, with enemies all round him, hungry for his property, thirsting for his blood. On the other hand, under the new law the chiefs, while they no longer had such reasons for cultivation of manhood on their lands, gradually or speedily lost the power as well as the will. When the clans were made dependent on the mere will of chiefs turned into lairds, there was no guarantee that the old family should retain the old patriarchal affection, or should remain in possession of the land. Those who did so, and strove to swim against "the stream of tendency," and retain the people on the land in the old fashion, ordinarily brought ruin on themselves and their families, while doing little good, if not harm, to the people. Others, with what to them was a veritable windfall of money, were ruined by extravagance, as of a poor man made suddenly rich ; others, by in-

competency to carry on business in a business fashion out of keeping with their training of previous habits ; others, by lack of adequate capital to carry on profitably their business of speculation in land. And hence in many cases where the old family has not remained, perhaps in a condition more or less of effeteness, the lands have passed into the hands of strangers, none of whom can know and love the clansmen as their chief, and some of whom may not care for any man but themselves, and, caring for themselves, naturally care much for sheep and deer.

For a sample of the result, let us look at the case of Glenelg ("Vale of Beauty"), whose wild loveliness flashes out, as of a fairy princess glancing shyly from the window of a fortress, upon the sea voyager as he passes into Kyle Rhea, on his way to Outer Hebrides, through the romantic Sound of Skye,

Where the hunter of deer and the warrior trode,
To his hills that encircle the sea.

There you can see the process, in a disregarded extremity, under the hands of autocratic landlordism, of a nation's bleeding to death. The facts are digested in the editorial columns of the Glasgow Weekly Mail, April 28, 1883 :—

The parish . . . extends 20 miles from north to south, and about the same distance from east to west. At the close of last century the population of the whole parish amounted to 2746. The tacksmen and crofters possessed a large stock of black cattle and sheep. The soil in the valleys is good—part of a deep black loam and part of sandy soil—and in those days yielded large crops of potatoes, oats, and barley. The hills are green to the top, and afforded excellent pasture for sheep and cattle. There were only 31 paupers in the parish, and the inhabitants were as a whole living in comfort. But a great change began when the clearances took place, and were carried out in the most ruthless manner. Tacksmen, crofters, cottars, all alike disappeared. . . A single sheep-farmer from Ayrshire rents the whole of this extensive valley [the "Glen" proper] and the surrounding hills, which at the beginning of this century afforded a comfortable subsistence to a contented and well-to-do population of nearly 1300 souls. On the other side of the loch, which bounds Glenelg on the north, lies the extensive district of Kintail, from which the sheep-farmers and shepherds have been expelled in a body to make room for a deer forest to afford sport to an American millionaire.

And so, as Lord Belhaven said, when to his view Scotland ceased to be through union with England, "There's an end o' an auld sang." So it appeared to a true poet with a Highland heart and a Lowland tongue :—

At the silence of night's contemplative hour,
  I have mused in a sorrowful mood,
On the wind-shaken reeds that embosom the bower,
  Where the home of my forefathers stood.
All ruined and waste is the roofless abode,
  And lonely the dark raven's sheltering tree,
Where the hunter of deer and the warrior trode,
  To his hills that encircle the sea.

This is what has come of—

O, Caledonia, stern and wild,
Meet nurse for a poetic child !
Land of brown heath and shaggy wood,
Land of the mountain and the flood,
Land of my sires, what mortal hand
Can e'er untie the filial band,
That knits me to thy rugged strand ?

The hand, replies autocratic landlordism, of "an American millionaire," who wants "for a deer forest to afford sport" to his restless idleness, that "land of my sires" which once sustained the grandeur of the mighty Mackenzie, "high chief of Kintail." Picture to yourself one of the old chiefs ;—e g., Sir Ewen Cameron of Lochiel. Lord Macaulay will bid you find his picture in Ulysses, not the superlative "Artful Dodger" of dramatic poetry, but Homer's Odysseus ;—whose sheer indomitable manhood moves us more than the half-unearthly transcendentalism of Thetis-born Achilles ; who, under a surface of consummate sagacity and prudence cherished a spirit of adventure which was the realised ideal of adventurous (in his case literally "daredevil") Greek speculation ; and who to all this added in perfection the endearing homely virtues, of love to wife and child that twenty years of warfare and wandering could not quench, and kind considerate goodness to inferiors such that swine-herd Eumaeus loves and honors him far more than he loves his own life, and even the aged dog, that has not seen him for twenty long years, now, when he returns in the disguise of an aged and ragged beggar, flickers out the last feeble spark of its life in the endeavor to welcome his returning. Such is the ideal which the warm-hearted clansmen represent to themselves when they think of an old chief, like that other Lochiel of Campbell, with a following of men, whose "swords are a thousand, their hearts are but one." And now "look on this picture and on that." Enter Yankee, the "American millionaire," with his "almighty dollar ;" and lo ! *Exeunt omnes:* farmers, shepherds, sheep, and collie-dogs, all vanish

pell-mell from the scene, like a company of ghosts when the cock has crowed alarm.

The dramatic effect of "skedaddle" occasioned by the entrance of that wandering conjurer from over sea, gives one a pleasing sense of poetical justice. But that serio-comic effect must not lead our minds away from due contemplation of the really tragic aspects of that history. The history, for instance, brings into clear light, with a startling vividness, as in light of lightning flash (suggesting thunder - bolts), the real character of much of that regime of lairdocracy to which the nation has confided so much of its profoundly vital interest in manhood. Though the sheep-farm should economically be a good speculation—for them, and the deer-forest a better ; and though the money thus made should enable them to throw over the business a certain halo or "glamour" of grandeur ; yet morally the grandeur is merely theatrical grandiose. It hides a shabby and dirty performer, who, outwardly a fine or noble gentleman, really is—like a fore-staller in the corn market—a sordid speculator in human life, ready to sacrifice the manhood of a region intrusted to him by God, at the bidding of an "American millionaire," who happens to be the highest "bidder" in the market. Morally, what difference is there, except in favor of the enterprising American—no longer a slave-marketer—between that grandee and the most consummately "vulgar Yankey" that ever worshipped the Dollar ?

But the darkest aspect of the matter is not that anti-climax of moral degradation in the landowning seller of men. Nor is even the deep private tragedy of an eviction, in its bearing on the people sold out of their old homes, the blackest of the darkness of that aspect. We do hear with horror of such outrages, inhuman and ungodly, really murderous, upon families and individuals, as characterised the "Sutherland clearings" a generation ago, and on account of which a leading representative of the great man was tried for culpable homicide. and in popular estimation ought to have been hanged. But our natural horror in contemplation of undeserved sufferings of helpless brethren of human kind must not blind us to a profounder tragedy behind. By the sea-shore of Galloway, one day in 1685, aged Margaret Maclauchlan was tied to a stake within reach of the rising tide. As she wrestled in her death agony, "for Christ's crown and covenant," the mocking persecutors pointed out her torture to young Margaret Wilson, also doomed to die for that cause. And they asked her—*in terrorem*—to frighten her into apostacy, "What see you there?" "See," said Christiana, faithful unto death, "What I see there is Jesus Christ, wrestling in one of His members." For us, alas! when we look at such an expatriation as that of our kindred from beautiful Glenelg, there is no such conquering hope; but rather a sickening fear of "woe to the land" in which such a thing is made possible by law. But that which will strike fear into cowards may strike fire from the brave. And the fear itself may prove to be one of those that "kindle hopes," if only it lead men, through the veil of that personal suffering in desolation to an innocent and prosperous population, to perceive and ponder, until it burn as a quenchless fire in their bones, THE "fact," that the nation there lies bleeding—the British Empire, to which more than to any other Heaven appears to have entrusted the destinies of the earth and its peoples, has, in that unregarded extremity, been bleeding to death.

That may serve as a sample of the bearing of autocracy in landownership upon amount of population. The district, you observe, which has been so completely emptied of manhood, is one well-fitted to maintain, in decency and comfort, a numerous population of men of high quality, such as Dr Stuart was wont to find so cordially welcoming him and sumptuously entertaining him, on his way through the Highlands to college in his youth. There thus is no possibility of putting on this case the false face of assuming that the land given over to deer is not fit to maintain men. But now let me show you another picture from the present day's life, of the sort of land, and of economical condition, that may be granted to those men who are not absolutely banished from the country; and request you to [judge whether the lairdocracy can be trusted to make sure provision for high quality of manhood, though failing to make provision for due amount of population. Such a picture may serve to enable you to realise in your mind what sort of nursing "for a poetic child" is now-a-days given through the step-mothership of lairdocracy, by Scott's "Caledonia, stern and wild." To say that in beautiful Raasay, Johnson's "island of the Phaeacians," the good land is given to a sheep-farmer and the people are huddled together on the bad land, is not to convey a distinct realistic impression. In order to have that, you must look at a concrete case in detail.

Well, here is the picture I have promised to show. It is of our acquaintances the Lewis men. They, on account of a demonstration they had made on behalf of what is highest and best, were once, by an influential political paper, nick-named "the just men of Lewis." Their good character was thus attested, when insulted. But now let us look at their homes :—

The materials of the picture were furnished by a special correspondent, appointed this year by the Glasgow Mail, a widely-circulated paper of unquestionable integrity, simply to observe and report the facts, for the information of the public at home and abroad. The digest of those materials, from which I quote, was in the editorial columns of the Mail for the week ending April 28, 1883 :—

The broad fact that in this pendicle of Ross-shire there are over 1000 families living in crofts the rents of many of which are variously one pound, thirty shillings, and fifty shillings a year, sufficiently indicates the vital importance of the question [regarding the "state of affairs" "revealed"]. It is quite certain that anywhere within hail of civilisation or its ways, the bulk of these rentals do not represent the value of house accommodation at all fit for human beings. No proprietor whose estates lay exposed to remark from modern public opinion would dare to house his tenants in the way that these rentals suggest. [Here the article gives illustrative cases—*e.g.*] Angus M'Neill's house . . . a byre, "or rather a midden-stead," at the upper end, inside, with manure from one to three feet deep; a kitchen in the midd c, with a fire on the floor; and two box-beds at the other end; all without partition, and nearly without furniture :—is the picture of one house. [But observe, the rental, of, say, 30s per annum (!) represents the value, not only of the house, but also of the croft—as to which we read] From the ground . . . the crofter must either raise sufficient of the fruits of the earth to supply himself and his family with a considerable portion of their every-day food, or he and they must starve, or live on chari'y. Semi-starvation is chronic, and misery permanent. But something rather sterner than semi-starvation is present just now [threatening of famine. Here again the c.se.] . . A few fish-bones showed what sort of breakfast had been partaken of, and two or three uneaten skates, the charity of neighbors, was all the food in the house. No other food of any kind had been in the house for a week. This was not the hut of a savage in a newly-discovered island, be it remembered. It was the house of a respectable Scotchman, with a wife and five children. He is living in his usual place of abode, and his circumstances have just kicked the beam a little over its ordinary hand-to-mouth balance. As he is, so, in the main, are hundreds of families in the Lews at this moment.

"Meet nurse for a poetic child." Very! As they are in Lews, so are they in other parts of the Celtic Highlands and Islands of Scotland. Let us, for instance, take a picture from Skye, still more to vivify realisation by individualising. This picture has had the fortune to go before the civilised world in the London Times, and then to come all the way round to the Antipodes here, when I found it in the Oamaru Mail of July 7th, 1883. But what has given it this rare fortune is not anything of rarity in the original; but the accident of his having been examined on oath by Lord Napier of Ettrick, and the Royal Commission. Here he is :—
"Donald Nicholson. . . . described as a hale old man of 78 years of age." Mark in his case what hopes for the future our brave young Highlanders have from Caledonia, what rewards of virtue for her "poetic child."

"I was a crofter in Totescore, but I now reside in Solitote. I have no land now. They doubled my rent and L1 more. I offered to pay the double rent, but I would not pay the L1 more, and I was ejected. The ground officer came and turned everything out of the house, and the tacksman of Monkstadt sent round word that if anyone opened their door to me or let me into their house they would be treated the same next year. My son's wife and her two young children were with me, and we were all that night in the cart shed, and our neighbors were afraid to let us in, and were crying over us. There was plenty of meal outside, but we had no fire to make a cake. We lived in the stable all the summer. I could only erect one bed in it, and my daughter and son's wife and two children slept in the bed, and I myself slept on the stones. During a vacancy the Presbytery of the Established Church allowed me to enter the glebe. After that I got refuge in the house of a poor woman at Duntulm, and the factor challenged the tacksman at Duntulm for allowing the poor woman to keep me in the house. Mr Grant, the parish minister, supports me now. That happened five years ago."

At the conclusion of his story, the old man appealed to Mr M'Lachlan, banker, Portree, who acted as interpreter, to confirm the facts. In reply to Lord Napier and Ettrick, the chairman, Mr M'Lachlan said :—

"After he was put out of his house he entered the shed and then he entered the stable ; then an interdict was taken out against him, forbidding him to enter forever the houses or lands. Under stress of circumstances he entered the barn with his family. He was laid up for breach of interdict, and for this breach of interdict

he was fined 10s, with the alternative of five days' imprisonment. The expenses of the interdict were 18. Then there was a year's rent due, and in addition to that he was charged with 'violent profits,' which means the doubling of the rent for remaining in possession after the term. The whole came to L35 odd, which the man paid.

"Lord Napier. — But do you mean to say that that money was really exacted, and passed into the factor's hands ?

"Mr M'Lachlan. — Yes. I arranged with the factor for him, and advanced the money out of the bank. When the markets came round, and he realised his stock, he paid me every penny of it."

Here occurs a reflection. The state of things represented by that pathetic case must be far from unfrequent—e.g., in the homes of the "just men of Lewis." The Glasgow Mail says that no landlord would care to have tenants in such accomodation as is there given to respectable Scotchmen with their families if the life-long outrage were perpetrated in the lfght of public opinion. Well, why is it not in that light ? Why is not the nation effectively in Lewis, with the "bull's eye" of its justice ? Why are the cases of Angus M'Niell and Donald Nicholson, when unearthed by an inquiry, as startling strange to the nation as Schliemann's discovery of the remains of the murdered Agamemnon in his "gory bed" beneath the long-buried ruins of Mycenæ ! The tyranny of old Rome would let no man escape from its view. There was not an acre in the civilised world in which the fugitive could conceal himself safely from her vengeance, which would not be searched with a hundred keen eyes and a hundred armed hands. How comes it, then, that such lamentable evils, life-long and widespread, where the nation's men are living honest and laborious lives, are so completely unnoticed by the eyes of its justice and love, which ought to be all-pervading as the sun,—"And there is nothing from his heat That hidden doth remain ?" How comes it that their poor abodes are as "dark places of the earth," whose fulness of "horrid cruelty" is left to be discovered to the wondering "public" by the chance diligence of a newspaper correspondent ? Because the nation has neglected its own business, to see to due maintenance of men by the land. That state of things could not exist anywhere in the land for an hour if the nation chose to see it and forbid it.

Consider, again, the physical conditions of the human life you have been contemplating, and the native tendency of these in relation to quality of manhood. See what is that life, under the reign of autocratic landlordism, in Lewis and Skye and elsewhere in the Highlands. The occupant is not maintained by the land but starved by it. In search of a maintenance for himself and his children, he has to wander far over land or sea, like the crows or gulls, in order, through the hardest and worst-remunerated labor, to scrape together, if possible, and save, some little money, which he may bring home with him in the end of the season to purchase meal for his family, and pay (what is called) "rent" to his landlord. When the capable men and women have thus gone away, "to beg a brother of the earth to give them leave to toil," the wretched "farming" at home has to be done by incapables — married women, children, aged and infirm. One day in Skye, I said to a minister that the poor little skeleton of a pony, with which a woman and child were trying to work the land, which they had manured with sea-ware carried from a distance on their backs, that the ricketty little creature was not fit for the work; that he and they might manage, simply with their weight, to drag the flimsy plough, so as to scarify the soil, down the steep hill face, but that for the return movement upward they would all require to be carried. He answered that he had seen such a horse draw a plough that was tied to his tail. There, you see, is the final cause of a horse, or economical end of his tail in nature. So, miserably toiling, at home and from home, our men spend what we call their "life," in which "semi-starvation is chronic, and misery permanent." When they cannot do or find poorly remunerative work to supplement the "farm" produce, or when any little thing goes wrong with the crops, then they are thrown upon the charity of outsiders, making a spasmodic effort for prevention of famine, with pestilence at its heels. It is thus that we provide for high quality of manhood, in the best breeding ground for men under the sun. We drive away the ablest men, and starve those who remain; and wonder at the folly of the man who killed the goose that had laid his golden eggs! Truly, we are masterly economists.

Now take a parting look at the landlordism to which the nation has committed the trust that ought never to go out of its own hands. While the people are chronically half-starved, and public charity is relied upon as an insurance against starvation, the landlords are driving a profitable trade in sheep-farming or deer-foresting, under protection of a nation which they do not support, as the mouse does not support the cheese in which it has a home and a portion. And, in addition to that, they charge their crofters and cottars what is called "rent" — for what! For the hovels and patches of land that are called their homes. Why should they pay "rent" for these, beyond a mere tribute in acknowledgment of lordship or superiority in the landowner? They are not homes, such as will give due maintenance to men, but only like the nests of crows and gulls, a sort of geographical point of departure and returning to those who wander far in search of a maintenance abroad. The landlord has not built them these crows' nests. The houses as a rule are built by the people themselves, and ordinarily the patches of land are created out of nothing but mere "waste" land by them—one of whom, after he has created a small farm with heavy toil of some years, can be turned out of it at any moment, with no "compensation for improvements," at the mere nod of the landlord or his factor. When, then, they pay for their holdings what is called "rent," it is not the whole truth that the land is not maintaining them. . It is another part of the same truth, that it is not maintaining the landlords. The landlords are maintained in part, either by the slavish toil of their so-called tenants in scraping together a "rent" from the lowlands or the sea, or by that public charity which is relied upon as an insurance against famine. That is what enables the tenants to pay so-called "rent" when the wolf is only at the door. And therefore into that so-called rent there enters the infamy of a pauper dole to the landlordism which, with "a hundred pipers an' a', an' a'," struts about in glory—so shameful.

Than such a deep, of despicable meanness of grandeeism, can there be a lower deep? I spoke of the gentility of that grandeeism, come in place of the simple grandour of old chiefs, as tending to slide into shabby genteel. Has it not slidden into shabbiness inexpressible? Ah! it is not only in the persons of crofters and cottars that the nation is undergoing degradation in quality of its manhood. Delenda est Carthago. Abolish for ever that autocracy of landownership which has made it possible for an honorable order of Scottish gentlemen to sink, inadvertently, into a gilded pauperism so vile—to maintain a shameful grandeur upon the lives of poor dependents, who themselves are dependent on charity of strangers! Surely, surely, "there's something rotten in that state."

One can regard with real sympathy, and even a sort of respect, a certain proud reserve of misfortune, on the part of old families incapable of dealing with the new situation, and disdaining to appeal for comfort to the sympathies of the commonalty. In that reserve of manly pride, even when it goes to the extreme of restraining from expression of natural sorrow on account of the misery of others, there is a certain grandeur, though it should be a savage grandeur—as when Cesar or Agamemnon covers his face with his mantle, or Outalissi will not wail, though he mourns, with Albert :—

As monumental bronze unchanged his look,
A soul that pity touched, but never shook ;
Trained from his t ee-rocked cradle to his bier
The fierce extremes of good and ill to brook,
Impassive—fearing but the shame of fear—
A stoic of the woods, a man without a tear.

Such an aspect might not, in meet circumstances, ill become the descendant of that old chief, who scornfully kicked away the snowball on which his son had laid his head to sleep, indignant at having lived to see the day when son of his was so far gone in effeminacy as to make use of a pillow. It thus is conceivable that a territorial grandee, looking on the desolation of the people entrusted to him, should be restrained from utterance of tearful confessions and lamentations, by a pride of manhood which is not unmanly though unnatural, like that of Prometheus chained to his rock, who will utter no cry of pain while the vultures are rending his bowels ; and be sustained in the unnatural hardness by a sort of perverted ancestral *noblesse oblige* :—

E'en from the land of shadows now,
My father's awful ghost appears,
midst the clouds that round us roll.
He bids my soul for battle thirst—
He bids me dry the last—the first—
The only tears that ever burst
From Outalissi's soul ;
Because I may not stain with grief,
The death-song of an Indian chief.

But, woe's me!—the pride now in our view is a pride that can stoop to live upon the misery of dependants, and to wring from them a part of the pauper dole of charity, making spasmodic efforts to save them from famine ! That pride you may call a "Heilan' pride." But in this case it is a low and dirty thing, vile and malignant as the poison that swells a serpent's loathsome head, and meriting the doom upon that "old serpent" in Eden, "Upon thy belly shalt thou go, and dust shalt thou eat all the days of thy life." In

reading the history of the Stuart Kings of England, and of "Bonnie Prince Charlie " after he had got safe away from the ruin which came upon so many in his cause, one is struck with the debasing effect of despotism on the despot. Plato's awful description of a tyrant's heart, as gashed and torn by passions, is to me less awful than the view of that heart simply hardened, "past feeling," so as to regard all sacrifices and sufferings of dependants as mere matters of course. Such, in relation to landowners of large estates, is the native tendency of that autocracy or absolutism of property; for the existence of which there is no real need in the nature of private property of any sort, and which had no existence in relation to private property in land until it stole in recently as an inadvertent innovation upon our national constitution, so as to be constitutionally only the unfortunate "accident of an accident."

You can see I have not formed my view of the state of things from abstract reasoning about the native tendency of a system, but have only generalised from observation of the system as it works in actual experience of life. And my view is not that of an isolated enthusiast, creating for himself a theoretical "idol of the cave." It is the view taken by men of affairs, who have eyes in their heads and hearts in their bosoms. The following statement was published within this year in the leading periodical of the capital of the Highlands (Inverness Courier, March 22, 1883). The writer (Scotus) is evidently a very able man, and seemingly an honest one. But we need not enquire about his character, for the statement speaks for itself :—

Those who are practically acquainted with what has been going on in the North for the last half-century are aware that the crofters' grievances . . . . , soive themselves into the irrepressible question of pasturage, without which, nature and local circumstances plainly teach, no rents can be earned in a region so elevated and exclusively pastoral. That again involves the necessity of a searching inquiry into the moral and economical consequences of large sheep runs, that have resulted in the serious deterioration of our mountain pasturage, and in the diminution of our flocks (notwithstanding an extensive resort to low country and artificial feeding in winter), and of those deer-forests that render a full third of some of the best grazings in the Highlands practically a mere waste, as useless as the ahara; where neither men nor useful beasts of the field are permitted to have a home or an abiding place, lest they may interfere with the amusement of 'the soft Saxon,' who shoots down a few half-tame animals in autumn, and calls it 'sport.'"

The deer forest we already know as land effectively insulated, or, for working purposes, sunk beneath the waves. Of the extent of the solitude thus created for sportsmen, where there well might have been men for the nation, our witness says, "a full third of some of the best grazings in the Highlands"—a statement somewhat misty in form of expression, but sufficiently impressive in substance of intended meaning. That great sheep-farms make the pasture land worse instead of better, and consequently make the productiveness smaller instead of greater, and in effect is thus a sort of "scalping" grandiosely,—this may be news to some of you, though I suppose it is not to practical men of land-cultivation. But observe that with such sheep-farming the nation is, in respect of economy, living on the capital of its life,—while the landlords may be thriving on the ruin thus involved in it. The witness is not before us on his oath. Personally I have no doubt of the substantial accuracy of his statement. But before you I lay it only as a representation, of what may be, and is credibly alleged to be, the state of things over the Highlands as a whole, under the reign of autocratic landownership. Is that a possible state of things? No honest able man who knows the facts will deny that it is actual. Every man in the use of his senses must perceive that it is possible. Well, then, for argument's sake, suppose it to be possible; think of it as conceivable. The possibility, fairly considered, will enable you to see *how* the population of the Highlands, though larger than it was some generations ago, may be less than half of what it ought to be now.

But, you still may think, that requires a process of reasoning; and a question like this,—What ought to be the population of a country, all things considered?—is, not one for mere argument by clever men with their spectacles and books, talking like students in the cloisters of a college debating society. It is a question for an experienced man of affairs, with wide and deep personal knowledge of such matters in the Highlands, and a well-approved solidity and strength of judgment, as well as unquestionable impartiality. Very well. Here is the very man you desiderate as judge. If there be one man of our time more than another whose judgment would be universally owned as the weightiest by all classes in the Highlands, whether tenants or landlords, or friends of both, that man of men for your purpose was the late Mr William Mackenzie, of Auchindinie, the famous factor of Ardross, whose beneficent skill, enterprise, and success for the landlords, as well as wise benevolence toward all, must be known by reputation to not a few even here at the Antipodes. Of him our witness justly says that he "was admittedly the highest authority in the north on that subject." And here, on your question, is the judgment of that authority, "admittedly the highest":—(*ut supra*, Inverness Courier.

He [Mr Mackenzie] declared to me that were the lands under excessive sheep pasturing, and the vast tracts occupied, to no good purpose, by deer forest's, divided into moderate-sized joint-arable and pastoral farms, with a mixed stock of sheep, cattle, &c., or into those club-farms which are productive of such markedly beneficial results on the estates of Sir Alexander Matheson—alike to tenants and owners—the county of Ross alone is capable of maintaining in comfort double its present population, and producing corresponding agricultural and pastoral results.

This judgment—of a great acknowledged expert—has immediate reference only to Ross-shire. But on this account it is all the stronger for our case in relation to the Highlands as a whole. Ross-shire is in its eastern part, by benefit of the balmy gulf stream climate, a richly cultivated lowland, part of "the garden of Scotland." According to Mr Mackenzie, the population of the wilder *half* of Ross-shire could, by reasonable improvements on a semi-barbarously wasteful mode of occupancy, well be raised so as to double the population of the county *as a whole*. But other parts of the Highlands have no such "garden" lowlands, already well-peopled, to counterbalance the solitude of their unreclaimed wilds. Consequently, of the Highlands as a whole the population well might be, and therefore ought to be, not only twice as large, but considerably more than twice as large as it is.

Observe that Mr Mackenzie, as well as the writer I have quoted, not only believes, but regards as unquestionable or unquestioned, that replacement of human population to a due extent in the sheep and deer solitudes, while of course it would add to the strength of the nation, would at the same time directly add to its wealth. Mr Mackenzie also holds, that the landlords would be really enriched by the process: that the excessive devotion to sheep and deer is for them a killing of the goose that lays the golden eggs. That, however, does not much concern us. What does concern us much is, that the nation, even in respect of material good, is directly made the poorer by the process of that devotion. It needed but this to complete the condemnation of landowning autocracy, now under trial with a witness and a judge, and therefore on the way to be found wanting as a public enemy. The system has not only wrought wofully ill to the nation all round, but under it the nation is now barbarously scourging the land, directly living on the landed capital of its life.

But what is the use of blaming the men for that? It is not the result of any evil taint in the blood peculiar to them. They are naturally of the same flesh and blood as their neighbors. You and yours would have been no better than they if you had been in their place. It is not the men that have made the system; but the system has made the men, or unmade them, if you will. Precisely. That has been my contention from the beginning, as it is my hope to the end. The system - autocracy in landed property—is at the root of those evils. It is idle to go lamenting and pottering about the fruit. To the root of the tree the axe must be laid. The system must be destroyed, so that nevermore it shall be out of nation's power to provide effectually for applying the land to its fundamental use, due maintenance of men. That may cost money to begin with. So does the "clearing" of waste land for cultivation. So does the fencing and drainage of a farm. So does the ploughing and sowing of one spring. Shall we grudge the cost of retrieving what the nation has lost, and providing for its future prosperity, in respect of that manhood which is its fundamental wealth—the root, the living foundation of all the nation's prosperity and life? Rather than suffer human beings to live under conditions unfit for manhood, the cities of Edinburgh and Glasgow have, at their own expense, demolished whole streets and quarters, worth far more than the whole estate of many a grandee. We paid 20 millions of pounds for the freedom of black slaves in the West Indies. Shall we grudge the cost that may have to be incurred for the existence of free white men, under conditions compatible with due maintenance of manhood, in the sacred motherland of free institutions and nations. If we grudge it now, we shall have to pay it again, with compound interest, as surely as God lives and reigns in righteousness, or there is any reign of righteous retribution in the history of nations.

But why have you not spoken of the great question about compensation to landowners, until you now have come to "the sentence after the last?" Because it really belongs to the place after the last. Interested parties have given it, and inadvertent listlessness has allowed it, in the discussion of the land question, a place of prodigiously exaggerated importance. In comparison with the real and great interest at issue, the nation's transcendentally great interest in manhood, the question about compensation is a characteristically paltry bagatelle of a side question. Still, as it is in the air, and may occupy and trouble honest men desiring to know the truth and do the right, I will now say a few words about that question.

The settlement I have suggested would destroy the absoluteness of private property in land. That absoluteness, we have seen, is peculiar to land, and affects the nation's great interest appreciably only in the case of great estates. And the owners of those estates have a peculiarly great interest in the peace and general prosperity of the nation. The skilled artisan, or hardy rustic or seaman, can hardly fall, anywhere or anyhow, but on his feet: he carries his fortune always under his hat. But as for the great landowner's greatness, any whirlwind of war or revolution might scatter it like chaff, while apart from an orderly society of mankind, civilised and tolerably prosperous, his land would be to him only what his land was to Robinson Crusoe. Further, as may be seen in the history of landed property itself, the innovation of autocracy in private property is contrary to good public policy of nations, or natural rights and duties of society as a whole; and therefore the autocracy can never attain to any footing in constitutional law, nor right in constitutional principle to be maintained in being by the nation—as if it had been founded on Parliamentary abrogation of the eighth commandment of the Decalogue. Still the innovation is a fact. Rightly or wrongly, the autocracy has the sanction of custom which makes law, and of legislation proceeding upon this law as making positive right, so long and so unquestioned as to have, let us say, materially augmented to be market value of the property. And to the extent of that augmentation, the market value of the property will be diminished by the settlement now proposed, in destroying that absoluteness of property or autocracy of ownership. Further, the present proprietors cannot in justice be regarded as themselves, exclusively or distinctively, the guilty authors of the innovation. No matter.

how it originated at first, the whole community, by its law and practice, had made itself responsible for the innovation long before the existing owners of the land were born. Hence, it may fairly be reasoned, the proposed settlement, in so far as it diminishes the market value of their land, will toward them be an act of confiscation, unless they receive compensation; a compensation which falls to come out of the nation's public purse, because the deed is done in the nation's public interest.

Now, so far as I know, there was no compensation made, nor thought of, to the clansmen, when their property was destroyed by the dissolution of the tribal ownership of clan lands. Nor was any compensation made or thought of to the commonalty of England when the "commons" were enclosed, and turned into private property of landowners. In relation to both classes of men, the nation's deed was one simply of confiscation, from the weak by the strong, in favor of the class who now are owners of the land. No doubt it was best for the whole English people that the "common," which was another name for "waste," should be made productive, and become a fruitful field of remunerative labor. And the Highland clansmen had an interest in common with other citizens in the good results of abolition of the clan system, with its evils of semi-independence re central Government, and the consequent insecurity of peace and order, both to the clans themselves and to the nation as a whole. Such consoling reasons of State necessity or general economical expediency might not be highly appreciated by the English working classes when every tenth man of them was in the workhouse; and may not be by the clansman of our day, when he has, perhaps, to leave a bed-ridden parent perishing with hunger and cold, in order, with wife and children, to wander and prowl along the desolate sea-shore, in search of shellfish or of carrion to keep famishing body and soul together. And, though they should now consent to starvation as martyrdom, or to emigration as "leaving their country for their country's good," still the fact remains, that to their class, when its property was being destroyed, and the proceeds handed over to the ruling class as a free gift, there was no word nor thought of compensation.

Still, compensation in such a case has at least an air of justice, as well as generosity. And compensation is made to Maori savages when their interest in landed property is made to give way to some

public interest of the nation. The nation may think it right to deal with noblemen and gentlemen owning lands in the Highlands, not as it has dealt with Christian Englishmen and Scotchmen of low degree, but as it has dealt with Maori savages of every degree. And perhaps, in its way to making the compensation there may be found no insuperable difficulty, through impracticable stubbornness, "more than perpendicular," of that perfectly disinterested public spirit in relation to money matters, which we have supposed, for argument's sake, to occupy the whole heart of all Scottish landowners in all times. For Dr Chalmers said that there are two things in nature which never change—"the fixed stars, and the Scotch lairds." And as a class they have not heretofore shown any disconcerting and baffling sensitiveness of bashful backwardness about receiving such compensations. They did not, for instance, evince any agonizing sensibility to the shame of accepting a free gift of the property which, without compensation, had been confiscated from their clansmen, in compensation for their loss of dignity and power through the abolition of the hereditary jurisdictions,—which really were not theirs, but properly a public trust from the clans. Again, they as a class held a public trust in the presentation to ecclesiastical livings, or patronage of churches. Some of them dealt with these as if they had been personal interests, and in this spirit battled for them as for dear life, at the cost of a fateful disruption of the union of Church and State. The burden of this public trust, they have been manifestly more than willing to undergo;—as if it had been for them a "burden that is light"—and on occasions of their being relieved of it, they have accepted compensation for the relief (from an onerous public duty) since the Reformation, not only once, but, I think, really three times. Possibly, then, the nation may find no difficulty, in the shape of over-scrupulosity in them about accepting compensation, to prevent it from relieving its own conscience by doing all that rigorous justice could exact for them. But when a great public interest of the nation is concerned, the feelings of that class must not be allowed to determine or to influence the nation's action relatively to the main question;—as compared with which—as I have said, this question about compensation is only a characteristically paltry bagatelle of a side one.

Now let me say a closing word to kindred Celts, about a matter which, sprung out of that clan system in which they have a peculiar interest, yet has a common interest for all. I refer to a certain sentiment of right, to something like permanent occupancy of their holdings, on the part of the existing occupants of cottages or crofts or small farms, in the Highlands. In Ireland the grievance on this account is, characteristically, in blundering patriotism, complicated with a semi-political grievance, against the Saxon oppressor, on the score of his having ousted from ownership the old Irish lords of the soil. In the Scottish Highlands the grievance, in relation to personality of ownership, is rather the other way ;—that the person by whom the people are now oppressed is their own kinsman, the representative of their old *ceann-cinnedch*, "family head," patriarchal chief of the clan ;—*et tu! Brute. His* being the person from whom the oppression comes, is to their feeling a peculiar aggravation of its bitterness ;—" that was the most unkindest cut of all." Further, in the Glendale case there has been, on behalf of certain pasturage occupied in common, a contention on the ground of some recent covenant, between Lord Macdonald or a recent predecessor and the people of the township. But deeper than that, in the mind and heart of their class in Skye and elsewhere, there is that sentiment of right I have spoken of.

The right here in the people's view, in Ireland as well as in Scotland, is specifically distinct from that natural right, which some have claimed for all men as men, on the ground that the whole earth is the common inheritance of mankind as a whole. The right of which the Highland crofter thinks is, not thus natural, but distinctively and emphatically positive. It is not a common right of all men as men, but a special right of the existing occupants of this piece of land. And the ground of it is not that all the world belongs by nature to all descendants of Adam conjointly, but that this particular district of the Highlands was, before the chiefs were made lairds, owned distinctively by a certain sub-division of a certain branch of the clan Japhet.

Now the very existence of that sentiment, with an historical occasion that may naturally have led honest simple men to entertain it, entitles them to receive from us, or at least binds us to bestow on them, a certain sympathetic appreciation of the moral quality of their contendings ; so that,—*e.g.*—though it may be necessary to the good order of society that they should not be allowed unpunished to take the law into their own hands, yet for a formal transgression of it

they must not be regarded nor treated as mere thieves, or robbers, or lawless filibusters. Further, apart from particular occasions of painful trial and perplexing and perhaps irritating difficulty, the history of the Highland population as a whole in relation to the land, and of the manner in which that interesting and virtuous population has been brought into deplorable ill condition, lays the nation under peculiar stringency of obligation to devise and to execute whatever measures may be best fitted to relieve the people from that condition ;—carefully remembering that this is the purpose to be kept in view, and not merely our deliverance from sentimental pain in seeing human suffering through woful want ; and that there may be a kindness which is selfishness or cruelty disguised—witness Isaac Walton's precept about impaling a frog as angler's bait, " Do it gently—as if you loved it." But all this is clearly short of even beginning to satisfy that sentiment of right. The sentiment will not be satisfied short of conceding a permanency of occupancy to those now holding the crofts and cottages. And my own view is, that to speak or think of this satisfaction to them as a settlement of the land question, is perfectly idle, and worse than idle. To do right in that way is simply impossible ; and, right or wrong, the establishment of existing occupants in a perpetuity of tenure would be no real settlement, nor beginning of a real settlement, of the land question as bearing even on crofts and on cottages.

That there ought to be crofts, cottages, pasturage, wherever that is desirable for the nation's public interest in manhood ; and that it ought to be an abiding burden upon all property in land to be available for that purpose on terms which the nation may see to be reasonable, and to be such that the occupants shall be able to live in decency and comfort ; this I not only admit, but regard and maintain as essential and fundamental to right settlement of the land question for the nation as a whole. But this would imply that the settlers, while thus enabled to obtain land worth keeping and able to keep them, would pay for it a fair market price, either as a round sum for freehold or as an annual rent for leasehold—would pay, that is, at least a minimum price to be named by the nation through its representatives. But the satisfaction I have spoken of, to the sentiment of right in the heart of existing occupants, would, on consideration, be far from being a satisfaction to other poor men who may wish to occupy land. Its effect would be that they and theirs would be excluded from the possibility of settlement on the land, at this time, or, indeed, in any future time. And to compel the landlord to give permanent occupancy, not for a price which the nation deems fair and reasonable now, or afterwards at recurring periods for reconsideration of rent, but for the price which the occupants may happen to have been paying in the past, and which may be far beneath real value now or in the future—this would be an effective confiscation from him ; which perhaps might be ventured on, as violent remedy for violent disease, in some extraordinary condition of terrible crisis ; but which, for permanent settlement of an ordinary matter of national business, would be simply bad administration of national affairs—present incapacity weakly sowing the seed of future disaster.

Broadly regarded, the process of satisfaction in that manner presents two aspects of sheer impossibility. On the one hand, relatively to the now existing landed owners. Remember that these existing owners personally had nothing to do with the dissolution of the tribal ownership of the clan lands. These have now been private property for a time so long as itself would have made ownership by right of possession. In the meantime, the property may have changed hands by purchase, perhaps repeatedly. And besides, it must have greatly changed in value, perhaps through improvements making the land a highly manufactured article. To claim the the aforesaid satisfaction, therefore, for the existing occupants on the ground of that old tribal ownership, would be to perpetrate a confused unreason of injustice, as if one of you were to claim the perpetual use of my coat, another of my plaid, &c., on the ground that some of your great great grandfathers were joint owners of a flock, some of which were probably the remote ancestors of the sheep from whose fleece those articles of mine have been wrought by the spinner and weaver and tailor. The more closely you look the more clearly you will see "impossible" here. And this leads to the second aspect of sheer impossibility. That is—

In relation to the existing occupants.— Suppose we try to distribute the old tribal inheritance, or a fair proportion of its present value, among them, so far as they really represent the old clansmen, and consequently are their heirs at law or in justice. We shall find it impossible to take so much as one real step towards that end in our view. In the case of the Maoris of the North Island, "individual-

ization of titles," though it may be difficult, is not impossible. For their tribal ownership of land is a fact at this hour ; and the individual's fair proportion of the proceeds of a sale is a thing that now admits of judicial investigation and ascertainment, by just men in Land Courts, assisted by skilled lawyers, on the ground of evidence accessible and producible. But the tribal ownership in the Highlands is a thing of the remote past. In law and in fact, every vestige of it passed from being 150 years ago. How, then, by the aid of a dim shadow of it now haunting the memory of day dreamers, could you seriously set about distributing, if you had it, the inheritance of the old clansmen, in fair proportions, among their heirs now in life ? The existing occupants of crofts and cottages—are these, alone, demonstrably, and in clearly ascertainable proportions, the heirs of the old clansmen ? Some of them may not so much as bear the name of the clan ; others may not have so much as one drop of its blood in their veins. There may not be one of them of whom it can be proved that any forefather of his ever had any distinct right to a share in the common estate. And then, as to the whole body of the real scions of the clan—Who are they ? What are they ? Where are they? Some of them, sprung from minor gentry or tacksmen of the old time, and now in positions corresponding to those of their fathers, are apparently by philo-Celts to be put out of the reckoning, and probably would make no claim for a share of the spoil, although as a class they should have the clearest and strongest right to it. As to the descendants of the old commonalty, some of them are now settled on other lands in the Highlands ; some are simply "landless, landless"; some are in the Lowlands ; many, far over the salt sea :—the now living clan are dispersed to every wind of heaven, over every quarter of the earth. Who is to find them all out, and identify them all, and show clearly what would fall to every one of them in an equitable distribution of the estate among them all ? No one. Not all the lawyers in New Zealand, or in the British Empire, or in the world. Not thousands nor millions of "wandering Jews." The thing is a manifest and utter impossibility. For working purposes of real life it has to be dismissed as chimerical, a mere day-dream, an illusion which will prove unfortunate to the poor man who carries his dream into business of daylight ; and seriously to speak about which, is to put a fool's cap on any movement for settling this land question to any good practical purpose.

The existing occupants will of course guard and assert any special right they may happen to have, through covenant with the landlords, or through custom of occupancy, as under the old "custom of Ulster." But that has really nothing to do with settlement of the land question on a permanent basis of beneficence rooted in justice. In order to such a settlement, the existing occupants must be regarded simply as citizens in occupation of the land; having no more right to the land on account of the old clan ownership than is possessed in common with them by their neighbors who are not in occupation of it, and by their fellow-citizens of the nation in general. If the old clan have any true heir, that heir is not the body of persons who now happen to be in occupation of the land; but the nation, which is the true heir of all tribes that merge into into its unity, as well as, relatively to land, paramount lord over all. In short, the nation must place itself, as regards ownership or occupancy, in the same relation to the old tribal estates, now become the private property of lairds in place of chiefs, in which it stands to those English lands which once were "common," and are now made private property of landowners. That is, in effect, there must not be recognised any special right of any clansman to the land, on account of the accidental circumstance of his residence or birth ; but all citizens of the nation must be placed on a common level, of equal right. And the equal right, in relation to the land, which all citizens have in common, practically amounts, it will be found on consideration, to a right to obtain from the nation that settlement of the land question, for all time and over the whole face of the country, which is best fitted to promote the nation's interest in the land, especially its great interest in maintenance of men.

The Highlanders may think that, when thus regarded and treated simply as citzens, on the same footing with all their fellow-citizens of the nation, they are in some way impoverished in respect of a beneficial interest of their's in the land. But in this case the poverty is one that enriches. They are stripped of vain illusions, in order that they may consent and seek to be comfortably clothed with substantial reality of benefit. For, while it is worse than idle to think seriously of of being replaced in the position of the old clansmen, on the other hand, by casting away dreams into dreamland, and considering what now is best, in broad daylight of real things, for them in common with their neighbors, they, with the aid of their pathetic story of suffering and wrong, addressing the nation on reasonable and tenable grounds of appeal for all, may help their fellow-citizens in obtaining a good settlement for all, whose beneficent results shall at the same time be the greatest attainable benefit for themselves.

We must not think about public questions only in kilt and plaid, nor speak of them only in Gaelic. In this relation dismiss from your minds the vain imagination of reversion to the clan system. Keep the kilt, and the Gaelic, and the bag-pipe, for high and solemn festive occasions. In ordinary life be contented with being simply a citizen,—of the greatest empire under heaven. The Celtic mind loves to linger in the past. And a restoration of the past, with something like what you suppose to have been the clan system, may haunt you in your day-dreams. But see that you regard it only as a dream,—a beautiful dream, perhaps—but only a dream.

Ah ! broken is the golden bowl,
   The spirit fled for ever.

It will only bring misfortune on you and others if you allow yourself to regard it in any other light ; or allow it really to influence your practical thoughts, feelings, actions, relatively to this profoundly important question about land. The clan system was good for its place and time. Notwithstanding physical discomforts and privations which would now be felt intolerable by their descendants, the clansmen, though little blessed with " peace," and certainly far from " luxury's contagion, weak and vile," yet appear, under the endearing and elevating influences of patriarchy, to have enjoyed abundance of "health," and a fair measure of "sweet content." But though the system thus was good for its time and place, its time is in the past, "returning never ;" and its place is nowhere now, in that great empire in whose citizenship we have the privilege of sharing. Let, then, the irrevocable past—be past. Patriarchy, with its enchantments, is only for the childhood and youth of our race : nationalism is for its robust manhood. To the history of that past, with its beauties and glories, real or imagined, we look wistfully back, as manhood looks wistfully back to childhood and youth, while " distance lends enchantment to the view." But childhood and youth do not return. Manhood, with all its hard realities of stern disillusionment, is better than childhood or youth returning. While, therefore, we cherish, as matter of pleasing and not unprofitable sentiment, the recollections and associations of the close unity of the clan, let our real life be cheerfully given to the endeavor to enjoy, and worthily fill and adorn, our place in the wider, and far higher and nobler unity of citizenship in the nation. So shall we pass into the manhood of mankind ; when the clansman, brave as his fathers, sets himself bravely to confront and to deal with the existing situation, in which the clan exists only as a lingering tradition, and the nation is a grand reality, ever spreading toward omnipresence like that of the ocean. Towards that nation as a whole, if we will serve God, we must cherish and exercise the feeling which the poet expresses toward a part of it :—

Oh Scotia ! my dear, my native soil !
For whom my warmest wish to heaven is
    sent !
I ong may thy hardy sons of rustic toil
Be blessed with health, and peace, and sweet
    content.
And oh ! may Heaven their simple lives
    p event
From uxury's contagion, weak and vile !
Then, howe'er crowns and coronets be rent,
A virtuous populace may rise the while,
And stand a wall of fire around their much
    lov'd Isle.

Milton Keynes UK
Ingram Content Group UK Ltd.
UKHW040931180224
437992UK00003B/169